Praise

Finding God in a Culture of Fear

'Joanne Cox-Darling has a gift for storytelling, which she uses with great ability to do the difficult weave between the Bible and the world we inhabit. She does not flinch before the shabby hope-destroying culture all around. But she also does not blink before the audacity of the Bible. Readers will be glad when they pause to participate in her buoyant gifts.'
Walter Brueggemann, Columbia Theological Seminary

'In this beautiful book, Joanne Cox-Darling dares to imagine church as a playful, joyous, hospitable community, where prayer, creativity and social activism are valued; where the kettle is always on and evangelism isn't an argument; where healing and hope can be fostered in this anxious, wound-up, exhausting world. Read this book and you'll want in on this magnificent dream too.'
Michael Frost, Morling College, Sydney

'Joanne Cox-Darling has written an erudite and courageous, gospel-based guide for those seeking hope in these troubled times, with the intent of helping us find God in the midst of a culture of fear. The subject matter explored is deep and challenging and Joanne engages this with her considerable theological skills. This is a very timely offering that I warmly commend for careful and prayerful reading and reflection.'
Andrew Roberts, writer, speaker and minister; author of *Holy Habits*

'There is so much in this book that demands our attention. Hope as the antidote to fear is riven throughout in an engaging, challenging and kind manner. It is invitational, begging us to live life through all its facets, fuelled by the love of God, which casts out all fear. Joanne Cox-Darling doesn't sugarcoat things or provide us with easy answers, but rather encourages us to ask questions and to use our life experiences and all the "gifts" of Pandora's box to find God in a culture of fear. Use this book individually, with one or two others or as part of a group meeting periodically, and relish its riches.'
Christine Elliott, director of international programmes, Churches Together in Britain and Ireland

'This is a book about and of hope. It comes from Joanne's lived experience and equips us to live hopeful lives now. Compellingly written, read it and be hopeful.'
David Male, director of evangelism and discipleship, Church of England

'Rare and readable encouragement for every Christian who knows what it is to feel anxious, homesick, exiled and bewildered about living life today, yet won't give up seeking to change the world for good, with God.'
Martyn Atkins, superintendent minister, Methodist Central Hall, Westminster

'Every day we are bombarded by bad news. We need a renewed sense of hope. Joanne Cox-Darling helps us find God's vision and see our world through the lens of hope, a hope rooted in the love and goodness of God. I commend this wonderful book to you with enthusiasm.'
Mark Russell, CEO, Church Army

'If a survival handbook is going to be effective it needs enough realism to take the situation seriously, enough hope to point to a better future, enough wisdom to go beyond what everyone else says and to be written by someone who has lived the life, not just spoken about it. Joanne Cox-Darling lives the life and shares realism, hope and wisdom in a way that love and joy conquer fear.'
David Wilkinson, principal, St John's College, Durham University

'This is a book for our times. Everywhere we look people are fearful – for themselves, their families and friends, their nation, the church, the planet itself. There are no quick fixes, but Joanne Cox-Darling offers signposts to well-informed and practical ways of navigating the landscape of despair. A combination of personal stories, scripture and questions for reflection make this an ideal resource for study groups as well as individuals. And as a bonus, it's all written in beautiful prose.'
John Drane, University of the West of Scotland

'Words do things and this is a book that does what it says. Reading this "on earth as it is in heaven" manifesto, hope itself stirred within me. For those of us living as exiles in the culture of fear around us, this is a fresh, evocative and practical resource chock full of inspirational stories and practices of hopeful resistance. Get it, read it, try it. It might just change everything!'
Revd Rod Green, vicar, St Peter's Harrow

'Anxiety can rob us of life and hope. Joanne's survival handbook takes a glimpse beyond today's prevailing fear-ridden culture, enabling readers to journey towards the life-giving hope offered by a gracious, faithful and saving God. My wise friend and colleague gifts us with relevant theological reflection rooted in scripture, with characteristic honesty and a light touch. This is a timely resource for both personal reflection and group discussion. Fear not, this book will not disappoint!'

Revd Tony Miles, broadcaster, author and deputy superintendent minister of Methodist Central Hall, Westminster

'An anti-anxiety pill for the contemporary Christian.'

Jennifer Smith, superintendent minister, Wesley's Chapel, London

The Bible Reading Fellowship
15 The Chambers, Vineyard
Abingdon OX14 3FE
brf.org.uk

The Bible Reading Fellowship (BRF) is a Registered Charity (233280)

ISBN 978 0 85746 646 4
First published 2019
10 9 8 7 6 5 4 3 2 1 0
All rights reserved

Text © Joanne Cox-Darling 2019
This edition © The Bible Reading Fellowship 2019
Cover image © Mark Owen/Trevillion Images

The author asserts the moral right to be identified as the author of this work

Acknowledgements

Unless otherwise acknowledged, scripture quotations are taken from the Holy Bible,
New International Version (Anglicised edition) copyright © 1979, 1984, 2011 by Biblica.
Used by permission of Hodder & Stoughton Publishers, a Hachette UK company. All
rights reserved. 'NIV' is a registered trademark of Biblica. UK trademark number 1448790.

Scripture quotations marked 'KJV' are taken from the Authorised Version of the Bible
(The King James Bible), the rights in which are vested in the Crown, are reproduced by
permission of the Crown's Patentee, Cambridge University Press.

Scripture quotations marked 'MSG' are taken from *The Message*, copyright © 1993, 1994,
1995, 1996, 2000, 2001, 2002 by Eugene H. Peterson. Used by permission of NavPress.
All rights reserved. Represented by Tyndale House Publishers, Inc.

Every effort has been made to trace and contact copyright owners for material used in
this resource. We apologise for any inadvertent omissions or errors, and would ask those
concerned to contact us so that full acknowledgement can be made in the future.

A catalogue record for this book is available from the British Library

Printed and bound by CPI Group (UK) Ltd, Croydon CR0 4YY

Finding God in a Culture of Fear

Discovering hope in God's kingdom

Joanne Cox-Darling

To Sophia and Karis.

You make me want to help make the world a better place for you to enjoy.

Acknowledgements

Writing is never a solo endeavour.

Thanks go to the editorial team at BRF. I apologise for my misuse of semicolons.

This project is itself the product of two periods of maternity leave and a sabbatical from my vocation in the Methodist Church. I am grateful to the generosity of policies that have enabled me to read, think and write.

Thank you also to the congregations who have helped to forge my thinking into practice: colleagues, congregants and friends at Central Hall, Westminster, and Codsall, Brewood and Coven in Wolverhampton.

To friends and subversives who continue to challenge me, and journey with me as we try to make the world a better place – and the church a theologically reflective place – thank you. Let's keep striving.

To trusted confidantes who read through the early version of this manuscript, I remain ever grateful for your time and encouragement. Jen, Sheridan, Tim and Andrew – thank you. Should you ever meet in person, please know that you all said the same things and have made this final piece far better because of your questions, exclamations and gentle challenge.

To broadcasters who have shaped my thinking or entertained me during this creative process, thank you. This is especially true of Wittertainment ('hello' to Jason Isaacs), *The West Wing Weekly* (for all those times I need to believe that it could all be so different), The Church of the Resurrection, Kansas City (which has special acknowledgement for starting me on the route to chapter 4), and anything edited by the brilliant journalist Ira Glass. My world would be much, much smaller, and a lot less hopeful, without your influences.

I am deeply and humbly grateful to Jayson, who has shared in our parenting through the many meltdowns over deleted chapters, and mulled over illustrations and concepts with me late into the night. I love you.

Contents

Hope that is seen is no hope at all.
Who hopes for what they already have?
But if we hope for what we do not yet have,
we wait for it patiently.

ROMANS 8:24–25

1

An introduction

God is not unjust; he will not forget your work and the love you have shown him as you have helped his people and continue to help them. We want each of you to show this same diligence to the very end, so that what you hope for may be fully realised. We do not want you to become lazy, but to imitate those who through faith and patience inherit what has been promised.

HEBREWS 6:10–12

Hope is being able to see, despite all of the darkness.

Archbishop Desmond Tutu

This is a survival handbook.

This is a survival handbook for those of us who feel overwhelmed by the world we live in. For those of us who are afraid of any one of the myriad different things: debt, death, failure, annihilation, anonymity – even the ubiquitous 'fear of missing out' that just makes life so exhausting. It's a book for those of us living with the realisation that life is just a little bit broken. Or quite a lot broken. It's a book for those of us who are angry about the status quo and know that there is much more to life than this; isn't there?

This is a survival handbook for those of us who have given up on the self-help section of the library, because the books there aren't providing the answers to the questions I can't quite articulate or identify yet.

This is a survival handbook for anyone who is searching for an alternative view to the fragmentation of the 21st century. It offers a hope-filled resistance to fear, despair, decay and devastation.

This is your invitation to discover a gospel of hope and to live a life of hopeful resistance. Hope can be defined as living in the expectation that something will happen. There is something deeper within Christian hope; the consequences of God's design, Jesus' resurrection and the Spirit's work in the world are already happening in the present. Christian hope is grounded in our present, everyday experience, and it relies on the actions of a loving God. Our response to this is an opportunity to participate in bringing God's future into reality. Hope requires action in response; it is not apathetic.

The opposite of hope is not hopelessness; it's fear and despair. The world we live in is marked by fear. As I write this, counterarguments to Brexit are described as 'Project Fear'. British security has never been on higher alert, as we are gripped by the real and present danger of imminent terror attacks. Journalists are continually caricatured as promoting a 'fake news' agenda, designed to terrify the masses, themselves becoming physical targets. Our bodies are constantly in a state of anxiety, with high levels of cortisol and adrenalin causing long-term damage to our physical and mental well-being. The world is getting hotter – politically and through global warming. Pension pots are running low as the population age rises, and in turn those far from retiring fear the lack of provision. And, if creation catastrophe, global politics, political philosophy, propaganda, terror threat and our own physiology is not enough to stop us leaving our homes, we become crippled by our personal fear of failure.

How (literally) on earth do we find hope – or even God – in an age of fear? How do we survive? What are we hoping for, and how do we try to enable it to happen?

This book challenges our preprogrammed acceptance that the world is a scary, meaningless, ultimately painful place – a place from which we are looking for some sort of escape. This book presents instead a vision of the world that God both intended to bring and is bringing into fruition: a world of invitation and opportunity, of relationship and beauty; a world of mystery and (re)creativity, where the people of God are once again at the forefront of discovery and are the embodiment of hopeful resistance.

The context we live in is a fearful one, fuelled by influences both within and outside of our control. But this is not the end of the story; it is the start of a rediscovery of the story of grace, stitched into the fabric of the universe. Fear should not, and does not, have the final word, despite our predisposition to listen to its power and to be tempted and cajoled by its influence on our lives and our world. Scripture says, 'Perfect love drives out fear' (1 John 4:18).

The following chapters are an invitation to explore the deeper mystery of hope, which in turn brings us face-to-face with the nature of God, the character of Jesus, the playfulness of the Holy Spirit, the promise of the future and the present/future potential of the community of the Christian church. Each chapter uses biblical roots to explore hopeful resistance in an age of fear. This is then followed by a series of questions, which are intended for your own use or as a small group study resource. Hopeful resistance is not an individual pursuit, so you may want to read this book with a group of friends, in order to help you discern your calling in God's world.

Chapter 2 sets us on course, offering a description of the UK in the 21st century and an explanation of why such lived experience may perpetuate a culture of fear. If we are to live a life of hopeful resistance, another world must surely be possible. In order to discern the future, however, we must understand our past and our present. The premise of this book is that we are living in a culture of fear. As institutions crumble, living hopefully can be nigh impossible. This chapter begins to notice what a hope-filled existence might look like in a culture of fear.

Chapter 3 begins by searching for God's identity within a culture of fear and anxiety. Experiencing the 21st century can be like living through the pain and despair of an exile. This chapter explores this metaphor, and it begins to identify biblical models of response to this experience: subversion, exclusivism, assimilation and vision. The consequence of an exilic experience is that it is easy to both blame and deny God. This chapter seeks to explore how these four models of response enable us to notice God's character amid the chaos. Hope is ultimately found in the loving compassion of the creator God. The exilic experiences enable us to identify this even in times when everything else evaporates.

Chapter 4 asks what sort of future we are looking for. Christian hope is caricatured as a simple argument about what happens when people die. It becomes limited to an after-life conversation, rather than a before-death invitation to change the world. This chapter explores an organic response to the two questions, 'What happens when I die?' and 'Why did Jesus die?' To live hopefully is to nurture an understanding of the gospel that is ecologically sound.

Chapter 5 moves from a vision of the future to a more grounded exploration of Jesus' ministry. The gospels provide examples of Jesus' participation in the messier parts of life. Jesus' encounters with people are tactile and personal. He challenges those who exclude people on the basis that they are making a mess (of the law, of the local community or of the geopolitics of the time), and he goes out of his way to eat with diverse dining companions. Jesus' model of hopeful resistance is one of healing, boundary crushing and bread breaking. In turn, we are called to get our hands and feet messy too. This is 'messy church' at its richest, rawest and best.

Chapter 6 explores what hope looks like in the age of the Spirit. Hopeful resistance in the power of the Holy Spirit is about discovering the divine flow that transforms all things. It takes seriously the fact that the Holy Spirit is engaging in the world and transforming it for the better. The Spirit turns the world upside down. Hope is present in the here and now, and it will take patience and courage to lean into the divine flow.

Chapter 7 explores the vocation of the church as an active community of hope, and it begins to imagine what our future calling might be. If we are to discover hope for ourselves, and if we are to risk living hopefully today, what might be the implications of this for the ways in which we offer God's love to a hurting and fearful world? How might a cultural revolution continue to bubble up in resistance to the despair and spiritual poverty of our society?

May we find God in a culture of fear. May we explore together ways of receiving hope afresh and, in turn, find ways to live lives of hopeful resistance: lives lived with the divine command to get involved and to change the world for the better, right here, right now.

For God's sake, as well as our own.

2

Opening Pandora's box

'Meaningless! Meaningless!'
    says the Teacher.
'Utterly meaningless!
    Everything is meaningless.'
ECCLESIASTES 1:2

It is not about hope. Screw hope. You just wake up in the morning and you do the right thing today. That's everything. It is cold comfort, but maybe it is the only truth we have at this time.

Chris Rose, director, Amos Trust

There's an ancient fable, a tale told over campfires and dining tables; a story told to try to explain the start of something; an origin story about the beginning of things. According to this ancient legend, a young woman – Pandora – was given a precious artefact, a jar or box or something similar. Into this container were gifted talents: beauty, charm, creativity. Alongside these gifts and talents were also offered more complicated opportunities that could be used for magical, mundane or manipulative purposes: gifts like curiosity, deceit, fear and persuasion. Pandora was tasked with keeping the item safe, with one further and vital instruction: do not open the box.

Pandora was an inquisitive individual, and eventually succumbed to the obvious temptation before her. The seal was broken, and the promise Pandora made was shattered beneath her fingertips. Slowly at first and then with more force and speed, the gifts inside the box began to seep out. Sometimes the good ones, sometimes the bad ones. Pandora tried with all her strength to put the lid back on, but the more she fought, the faster they escaped. Pandora was faced with a new world, full of fear, mystery and malice. Pandora knew the world had changed and knew that it was her broken promise that had caused such a cataclysmic mess. Resigned to whatever fate may befall her, Pandora slumped back from the prized and precious artefact – ashamed, guilty and terrified: feelings new to her, having been unleashed from the container just minutes before.

It was only then that she noticed a glimpse of something in her peripheral vision. There was a single remnant of blessing in the box.

Sitting in the corner of the box, tucked away until the very moment it was needed the most, remained hope.

The final gift to Pandora, and to the rest of the world, was hope.

The 21st century is struggling with its own brand of box-opened chaos. Our experience appears fear-fuelled and hopeless. Turning the pages of newspapers, looking at headlines, watching movie plotlines and observing international relationships, we live in a tumultuous time. Listening to the stories of failure, pain and fear from friends, colleagues, family and even ourselves constantly demonstrates that we are out of control and struggling to keep everything together. We live in a time of increasing creativity and global networking, and yet it is also a time of great fear, shame and manipulation. Western society has tried to maintain the status quo, and yet somewhere along the line, just like Pandora's box, the seal was broken. The harder we try to put the lid back on, it seems the worse things get.

In a world ruled by fear, people are pinning their hopes on to different institutions to get us through. Time and again, however, we are let down and we become more afraid of what will happen next. Church denominations are faced with past and present cases of abuse. Some politicians barely survived an expenses scandal. Bankers found loopholes in practices which in turn contributed to a global recession. Charities have become the centre of investigations into the trading of favours among the most destitute of people. The film industry is tainted by powerful men taking advantage of people in auditions and performances. And when all these institutions begin to crumble, not even the hope of fame and fortune promised in reality TV shows can provide salvation for the masses.

Diagnoses keep coming. The pain is ever-present. The questions leave us breathless. Fear leaves us terrified.

And everybody hurts.

One in four people in the UK are prescribed antidepressant medication. One in two people will be affected by cancer in their lifetime. One in three women and one in five men have been sexually assaulted. One in six people have been abused as a child. Five people per day die in road traffic accidents in the UK; a further 61 are seriously injured. Police receive over 100 calls about domestic violence every day. More teachers leave the profession than are recruited into it, often citing targets and workload as the reason for their departure.

Everybody hurts.

It can be hard to hear the whisper – the whisper that another world is possible.

Hope is the catalyst in the midst of chaos. Hopes hangs out for things to be different. Hope doesn't take the statistics for granted. Hope whispers on the breeze that another world is possible.

This book is unapologetically Jesus-focused. We can hope in all sorts of things and people, but the ultimate start and end, the ultimate gracious paradox, is to be found in the Godhead – the creator, saviour and performer – of history, salvation and the kingdom of God.

We are surrounded by all sorts of promises made by people and by corporations, and yet little by little the hope that they offer is exposed as baseless. In Christ we discover a God who created the world and who constantly intervenes to build relationships and to transform the chaos with which we exist. In Jesus we discover the example by which a new world order is offered. In the Spirit we find the energy and drive and constancy through which a new heaven and a new earth are being shaped right under our feet. In relationship with this divine dance of life-breathing Trinity, we too find our place in this incredible story of hope in the midst of fear. Through the church we find a community of hope-filled rebels, struggling and striving to seek first the kingdom of God, and setting a new agenda for the future.

Another world is possible. It's not all hopeless.

I refuse to believe that this is it, although it is all too tempting to revert back to the strange comforts of a culture of fear.

I do not believe that creativity, beauty, happiness, peace and justice are lost in the midst of processes and procedures and the disruptions and pain of life. They are hard won and sometimes difficult to notice. But they are worth fighting for, waiting for, dreaming about. Humanity was not created for despondency. Fear is not the category that should shape our lives, our behaviour, our politics or our world. Humanity was created as the pinnacle of creation – as the very essence of God's love, care, vitality and beauty. Even our wrinkles, spots, stretch marks and weird toenails express something of God's delight in our communal existence.

Yet all too often fear and apathy are the strongest currency in how we experience the world today. It's the stuff of soap operas, and it's what sells newspapers. It makes our world smaller and reduces our influence. It is intoxicating and addictive. But it is not how we are meant to be living. It's just too exhausting. It's too hard.

There has to be an alternative. Hope has to remain, even if it is scrunched in the corner. Hopeful resistance is the invitation of all, and the vocation of the brave.

In our contemporary experience of life, it is possible to find some sympathy with the writer of Ecclesiastes – who was faced with the terror of feeling abandoned to the whims of local political powers that had ripped out the very heart of their community, with the emptiness of their religious practices, and with the apparent absence of a distant and vindictive God. In Ecclesiastes, it is tempting for us to find some solace in the parallel experience of anxiety and apathy:

> 'Meaningless! Meaningless!'
>   says the teacher.
> 'Utterly meaningless!
>   Everything is meaningless.'
> ECCLESIASTES 1:2

Meaningless. Worthless. Hopeless. Futile. Thirty-eight times, the writer defines their life experience as meaningless.

When all we know are temporary and unsatisfactory experiences, the response of the writer (and perhaps our response too) is one of scepticism, cynicism and complaint. When the world is a corrupt, pointless endeavour, one response is to become bitter and angry. Life, after all, is wearisome and full of trouble, and then you die. This can be a safe place to reside, wallowing in cynicism and world weariness rather than daring to resist the sense of futility and instead actively working towards a hopeful alternative.

Such anxiety and a sense of relentless doom also affects humanity's ability to notice God's involvement in the world. For the writer of Ecclesiastes, this leads to the conclusion that God is distant from creation and separated from the people. This is in part mirrored in the increased secularism of contemporary society.

Yet even the writer doesn't truly trust that this is the sole reality for the community. There is a flip side to the dialogue, as the writer still struggles to reconcile their knowledge and experience of wisdom and spirituality.

The writer then explores the *mist* and *vapour* of their culture and context, trying to find something of joy and hope in the midst of the frustration and routine. For the writer of Ecclesiastes, this hope is hard to come by, but it doesn't stop them from trying. Life is hard and complex. It is full of opportunities to keep busy and to be active, and yet none of these activities seem to achieve anything. There may be a time to dance or a time to laugh, but they are all fleeting pleasures in the midst of a bleak, cold world.

The writer desperately wants to hold on to something else, to present a more balanced approach rather than to drown in their own despair.

> Anyone who is among the living has hope!
> ECCLESIASTES 9:4

Hope weaves a different narrative into the chaos. Hope resists the melancholy. Hope restores the community to wisdom, to action and ultimately to worship. There is a combined response, even in the midst of a foreboding sense of meaninglessness. To press forwards into the future, there needs to be both activity and worship – that is, both trust in God's activity and a human response.

Ecclesiastes refuses to be contained and confined by the temptation to cynicism. Instead, the conclusion of the dour poetry is to cultivate contentment – to speak up about the frustrations of the present and to name imperfections where they are to be found, but also to be fully present to the current time and to discover peace and wisdom from within our surroundings, not despite them. Ecclesiastes is not about winning a fight; it is about discovering that hope is not a future goal but a present invitation to notice that even the simplest of things in life can make it worthwhile. There is, after all, a time for everything under the sun.

Whether we are engaging in a biblical survey of the vanity found in Ecclesiastes, a stark rendering of UK statistics or a narrative of the bankruptcy of contemporary society, there remains a choice: succumb to the disorder and chaos, becoming increasingly embittered in the process, or discover the balance that comes from naming the negative experience while holding the tension of knowing the hope of God's work in the world. There is an ancient/future dimension to hope that speaks the truth of the current experience but also allows for God's saving grace to bespeckle a future yet unimagined.

Hopeful resistance lives gracefully, beautifully, patiently in the present while striving towards, and actively building, a renewed future. It encourages action, where the world lives in apathy. It challenges meaninglessness with purpose. When the temptation is to live small, cynical, despairing lives, Christian hope is a vocation to speak up, act up, listen up and get up.

We catch our glimpses of hope in our peripheral vision, just as Pandora did – when there is nothing else remaining and when our inertia, melancholy, ambivalence or pain has won us over.

We hear hope, standing on the sidelines, cheering on our team at the crucial moment in the match.

We notice hope in the centre aisle as a couple prepares to say vows and to declare 'I do' before friends and family.

We trust that hope will be present in our own versions of 'happily ever after'.

We cling to hope in hospital wards and consulting rooms as we await diagnoses, prescriptions and plans.

We long for hope, alongside Pandora, watching for what remains in the corners of the broken vessels of our lives.

Hope is weaving and recrafting a new future out of an ancient past, which does not depend on our preferred or desired outcome, but which does invite our participation.

Hope is living faithfully in the present moment, while striving for the blessing of a future as yet unknown.

Hope is God's co-conspirator in the holy triptych of virtues: faith, hope and love. In turn it raises the question: what difference does hope make to love, and vice versa?

Hope has nothing to do with us; it has everything to do with God, the life-giver, the pain-bearer, the love-maker.

Questions for discussion

- To what extent do you recognise the description of contemporary living? What would you add from your own experience?

- What are you afraid of?

- When have you experienced life as 'meaningless'? What happened?

- What comes to mind when you think of 'hopeful resistance'?

- Is another world possible? If so, what might it look and feel like?

3

Feeling homesick

Those who hope in the Lord
    will renew their strength.
They will soar on wings like eagles;
    they will run and not grow weary,
    they will walk and not be faint.
ISAIAH 40:31

The people who know God well – mystics, hermits, prayerful people, those who risk everything to find God – always meet a lover, not a dictator.
Richard Rohr, *Everything Belongs* (Crossroad, 2003)

Houston, I've got a problem

I was three days into my first week away from my young family. Our daughter was nearly one, and she had just begun to discover the world by running. And climbing. And naming objects. In other words, she had just started to get interesting, having reached the end of the previous few months of feeding, teething and crawling.

I, however, was sitting in a hotel room in Houston, Texas, struggling to get the Wi-Fi to work well enough for an early morning (for me) Skype conversation. I'd survived the first couple of days through a mixture of culture shock, jet lag and soda from the nearby diner. I was one of a group of representatives at the World Methodist Conference: a four-yearly extravaganza of global worship, biblical exposition and whispered corridor politics, as the business part of the conference began to shape its agenda for the following week. I had been asked to preach the penultimate sermon of the week – an honour I did not take lightly and the script for which I had crafted over the best part of the previous year.

This third day was different. The preacher in the morning was a fabulously extroverted bishop from one of the southern states of the USA, and she had preached a phenomenally charismatic, Pentecostal-style rallying call. There were several standing ovations to her words, and her sermon concluded with a giant conga-line marching around the room, as people from around the world joined in a lengthy version of the chorus from the 1970s hit 'Love Train'. Surreal doesn't quite adequately describe it.

The pressure. The jet lag. The caffeine. Together the whole scenario became far too much for me. I melted in a heap of sobs, surrounded by my generous colleagues as they returned from their line dancing. In a very British attempt to maintain a stiff upper lip, I managed to smuggle myself into an elevator and headed to my room – a moment during which, with mascara and tears dripping down my face, I came face-to-face with some of the US Paralympic athletics team. Could the moment get any worse?

Crumpled in a heap in my room, I was faced with a number of realities. First, there was no way I could preach like the amazing woman who had graced us with stories, dancing and ovations – and a conga line. All I was hoping for was that a couple of people would laugh at the two jokes I'd written. Second, why was I here? Even in the USA, the language was different, the food was different, the music was different. In a global environment, such as at the World Methodist Conference, my sense of alienation was paradoxically perpetuated and yet normalised, as everyone joined together in a fiesta of perspectives, debate and colourful fabric. Third, I hadn't learnt the script for my sermon. No one else had used notes. I had ten pages of sermon material carefully crafted, but not yet transferred to prompt cards or to memory. Fourth, I wanted to go home. I felt a fraud in a room full of bishops and political representatives. I was a missiologist who preached a bit in the UK. I didn't have a place here. Fifth, I missed my family. I was even missing my daughter's scratching nails and her stubbornness, now she had learnt to say 'no'.

I was homesick.

I couldn't move for the fear of failure I had put myself under. I wanted cuddles not from colleagues (although they were lovely), but from my partner and my daughter. I wanted Yorkshire puddings rather than nachos, and lukewarm cola served in a can rather than ice buckets full of the sticky substance, refilled every time I took a sip. I wanted life to be back to normal and to be in a place where I knew the language and the routines and the music. And where I wasn't expected to join a conga line at the end of a sermon.

I wanted to go home.

I had never felt such a deep-seated response to being away before, and it took me by surprise. It fuelled every part of my psyche, which had a cumulatively negative effect on my well-being and self-confidence. It incapacitated me, and it stopped me from engaging with colleagues without crying. It was utterly exhausting.

Yet a few days later, my sermon had been preached well, the jokes had received appropriate responses from the gathered global community – I had even been cheered at a particularly poignant moment of exposition – and I had a return plane ticket. A few days later, I was home. Sweet home.

In the previous chapter, I described the experience of living in the 21st century, especially in the global north, in a somewhat stark fashion. The world has changed so quickly and on so many different fronts that it can be hard to feel secure and up to date. Day-to-day living becomes more about knowing how to survive rather than thrive, as if we are on some sort of reality TV show, desperately trying not to be found out or voted out of our comfortable existence. Technology, lifestyles, diversity and ideologies are all developing and conflicting around us, and we have a choice as to whether and where we engage.

It is tempting to retreat to the safety of our homes and favourite armchairs and to disengage from the fast-paced world in which we live. We can experience our contemporary society as an alien culture, threatening all our home comforts, and we may feel homesick for the world in which we grew up – our personal nostalgic vision of our childhood or young-adult experience that, even with rose-tinted glasses, seems on the whole a lifetime ago. Unlike my Houston experience, however, we do not have a return ticket. We will not be returning to the world we once experienced. The dance of progress continues, and it's in our power to decide whether we retreat, engage or find alternative ways of living and loving our way through life.

In this chapter we will explore this sense of cultural homesickness: the desire to be 'back home' when everything else is changing. The Bible explores this through the real and felt experience of God's people in exile, a time when there really was no going back, and the dislocation and despair felt by the people was devastating to them. In exile, it can be easy to deny God's existence, to remain apathetic and cynical about the world around and about us, and to wallow in the belief that things were better in a different time and place. However, to live hopefully is to find ways to engage with a new reality, to keep on changing, to face our fears and not to be cajoled into despair.

Amid the fear and challenge that such an experience perpetuates, it can be all too easy to begin to lose sight of God. We are taken in by the headlines and statistics about church decline, in both attendance and influence. We struggle to find God in worship, and our own faithfulness dwindles as we become unable to hear from God amid all the additional noise. We get cynical and bitter. Blame is apportioned at every opportunity, deflecting our personal insecurity through victimising someone or something else – and if all else fails, we blame God for not caring about the world anymore. Our prayers are not answered, at least not always in the way that we want God to respond. Our attention is grabbed by another programme or idea that will offer us a way out of this mess, without us having to change the very depth of our personal and communal character.

The good news is that we are not alone in feeling dislocated and isolated. There is hope.

Exile

The biblical scholar Walter Brueggemann has pioneered a significant shift in recent theological thinking. He proposes that one way to understand our contemporary situation is to see the Jewish experience of exile as a metaphor for the 21st century. This is not to say that contemporary Christians have been politically displaced (although some will have been), nor that we face fatal persecution from world leaders and antagonistic ideologies (although some will have had this experience). By using a metaphor such as exile, there is the ability to acknowledge pain, fear and despair but also provide the tools and models for hope. The metaphor offers the biblical tools and resources needed for us to move into a place of deeper mystery and presence or else to step away from the possibility of God's intervention and care altogether.

The metaphor of exile is primarily a pastoral response to the contemporary experience. Exile enables us to recognise that we are not alone and that our homesickness has been experienced before, in similar and deeper ways. We become aware that God knows our anxiety, fear, hopelessness and pain. It also means that there are already tools and resources in place to enable humanity to flourish, and for God to be involved and worshipped within the experience, rather than despite it. The exile metaphor gives us permission to react to our situation: to fight, assimilate, trust in something bigger, or try to change the situation for the better. As will be explored in this chapter, the Bible offers all of these alternatives as faithful, hopeful responses to the terror of exile. Exilic experiences risk being viewed as times of God's absence rather than intervention. By using exile as a metaphor, God's character is revealed to the hope-poor people: love, compassion, faithfulness, presence and peace – all have a place and offer the community hope in their despair.

Biblical exile

Having made assertions about the power of the exile as a metaphor in our own experience, we need to explore the implications and experience of the exile for those enduring it.

The Hebrew people were physically displaced during their exile experience, which began when the Babylonian rulers finally defeated Israel's army and became the dominant political and cultural force of the ancient Near East. With the defeat came the abandonment and desolation of the temple in Jerusalem – the central place of worship for the Hebrew people and the place where God's glory dwelt. Without a place of worship and with a defeated political system, the Hebrew people profoundly felt God's absence and were themselves dejected and defeated. Almost overnight they found themselves in a new place – a physical and psychological reality where the things that they valued the most were being destroyed and trivialised by a dominant cultural force that they had no ability to challenge or defend against. It was terrifying.

What began as a physical, geographic shift of identity quickly became an experience that overtook their social, moral, religious, political and cultural identity. The exile stripped the Hebrew people of everything they knew, and it destabilised their sense of community. In turn, God was seen to be at best apathetic and at worst the cause of their plight. The people thought that the exile was a punishment for their disobedience, but they no longer had the tools and resources to assuage God and to relieve them of their guilt and shame. It seemed that God had taken a leave of absence and left them to depend on their own devices in a strange and alien land. Yet, as every part of the community identity was exposed, in the heart of their vulnerability and despondency, the community was also able to discover God's true identity, to hope and trust God, and to understand God's mercy, love, compassion and grace.

As God's identity was reaffirmed, and as the community relocated their belief systems and cultural identity, so too were the people able to respond to God's calling upon them both as a nation and as individuals. The exile inspired poetry and prophecy not seen anywhere else or at any other time. Hope is found in the transformative love of God, present in the midst of despair.

It is this biblical exilic literature, this honest, brutal and daring exploration of faith, that provides fertile ground for a contemporary reading of exile as a metaphor. It is through the books of Lamentations, Jeremiah, Esther, Isaiah, Ezekiel, Daniel and Nehemiah that we are able to explore the nature of hopefulness, within the bitter reality of exile's loss and costliness. Hope holds the tension.

There are four different models of response that the Hebrew people made amid the pain and opportunity of their experience: subversion, exclusivism, assimilation and vision. Although not mutually exclusive, scripture offers each of these as a valid and valuable response to exilic experiences. In each of these models, there is the invitation to actions that offer a hopeful resistance to the status quo.

Subversion

This describes the realisation that life will never be the same again but that there are ways of influencing specific situations and people to enable the spiritual and social flourishing of the Hebrew people.

A good example of this subversive response to exile is found in the book of Esther.

King Xerxes was a gregarious ruler, displaying his wealth and splendour in opulent banquets and celebrations. Having been disrespected by his wife, in a fit of rage at such disobedience and in order that other women would not follow suit, Xerxes took the drastic decision to exclude his queen from his court. As his anger dwindled, so did his mood, and a search was undertaken to fill his courts with a harem of young women.

An orphan named Esther was among those entrusted into the care of the harem officials. She left the home of her uncle, Mordecai, and began her training within the king's court. Esther quickly became a popular and well-respected member of the court, and her training was fast-tracked to prepare her to meet King Xerxes. Throughout her training and beauty regime, Mordecai looked out for his ward and continued to encourage her. Crucially, he advised her to keep her cultural heritage a secret.

Esther not only gained favour with the court, but after ten months of preparation she also gained favour with the king – and soon became his new queen. The king threw a banquet in her honour, declared a national holiday and shared some of his wealth around his kingdom.

As queen, Esther had a privileged seat of power within the royal court, a position she was able to use well when Mordecai discovered a plot to assassinate the king. Esther continued to prove herself loyal to the king, while also maintaining her dignity as a Hebrew, an identity kept secret under the protection of Mordecai.

As power brokers rallied for more and more influence, a genocide was ordered of all Jews across the whole of Xerxes' kingdom, and Esther was tasked with changing the king's mind. Pleading with the Jews to pray and fast for her, Esther took her next opportunity to meet with the king, and in a spectacular turn of events, she saved the Hebrew people, and the court power brokers were condemned to the same fate they had planned for the Jews:

> In every province and in every city to which the edict of the king came, there was joy and gladness among the Jews, with feasting and celebrating. And many people of other nationalities became Jews because fear of the Jews had seized them.
>
> ESTHER 8:17

The story of Esther is one of subversion. It's a story of a clash of cultures that eventually sees the rise of the Hebrew people, despite their persecution and exile. It speaks of the importance of influencing power and speaking truth with modesty and courage. It's a book about discernment, dignity, wisdom and resistance of the status quo. The book of Esther recognises that people are raised 'for such a time as this' (4:14) and that leadership and the ability to change the world can be found in the most unlikely of people and situations.

Esther is a book of hope to an exiled people, because it is uncompromising in stating the value of God's people, as well as exposing the political mechanisms by which change happened in the time of King Xerxes. Esther subverted her position as queen, and in so doing undermined the plot to eradicate the Jews from the empire.

Hope can be found in resisting and subverting roles and experience, in order to bring about a new reality. There is integrity, dignity and authenticity at the heart of this account. It offers inspiration to those who are willing to give up everything in order to speak truth to power at the opportune moment.

The instigation of a new benefits system in the UK has been widely evidenced as having a negative impact on the very people it was set up to help. This has included an increase in the use of food banks and in the number of people living below the poverty line. In Gateshead, the introduction of the new system was scheduled for

November of that year. In the run-up to Christmas, churches were seeing an increase in local poverty. One local church leader decided to take a creative response to the situation and the season, inviting people across the country to 'be an angel' and send an angel to the prime minister and to their local MP, asking them to stop the implementation of the benefits system. From deep within a local situation, a subversive voice used a symbol of hope and of good news (an angel) in order to speak truth to power.

Exclusivism

Whereas Esther aligned herself with the political powers of the Persian exile, a second model of exilic response can be found in the account of Daniel. Rather than get mixed up in the cultural nuances of the kingdom, Daniel took a more exclusivist approach to his Babylonian protest, remaining faithful to his Jewish practices even when it risked his life.

Famous for its narrative of the lion's den, the book of Daniel is an unusual exilic text, as it merges prophetic witness with apocalyptic visions of end-of-the-world terror. Daniel's personal experience personified the experience of the Hebrew people and thus maintained the hope of a nation through remaining distinct from the culture around and about him.

The book begins with the fall of Jerusalem and the start of the Babylonian empire. King Nebuchadnezzar came to power, bringing with him some of the best Hebrew men to be trained in the ways of Babylonian culture, given language lessons and invited to improve their etiquette. Daniel and three of his friends were part of this group, and, with new Babylonian names, they began their cultural-assimilation programme.

'But Daniel resolved not to defile himself with the royal food and wine' (1:8) and set out to prove his and his friends' value by following a strict vegetarian diet. At the end of the test, Daniel proved himself to be stronger and healthier than all the other courtiers, and their request to have separate food was granted. Daniel and his friends proved themselves more worthy and wiser than any of the other candidates, and so together they stayed in the king's service.

In the first half of the book of Daniel, the same pattern of events recurs time and again: a royal decision is made, Daniel and his friends refuse to participate, they are punished, God shows up, the king recants. So, in chapter 3, we read that the decision was made to force all the people to worship a gold statue of the king, 60 cubits high and 6 cubits wide. However, Daniel's three Hebrew friends, whose Babylonian names were Shadrach, Meshach and Abednego, refused to follow the king's orders, and, as a consequence, were thrown into a fiery furnace. God proved faithful to those who remained faithful to God, and the three friends were saved. In turn, King Nebuchadnezzar repented of his decision, and the three friends received a promotion.

The famous story of the lion's den (Daniel 6) follows a similar pattern. The empire continued to thrive and to grow. King after king acceded to the throne, and Daniel proved himself faithful, especially in matters of divination and dream interpretation. However, Daniel defied the new King Darius' edict not to worship any other god except the king, and he became victim to a plot to get rid of him. Daniel was discovered worshipping God in private and was condemned to death. King Darius remained troubled by the decision and was the first person to attend to Daniel following his night with the lions. The king discovered that although he had condemned Daniel, Daniel's God had protected him, and thus Darius witnessed God's faithful provision to God's chosen people.

As a result, the whole kingdom was invited to worship Daniel's God – the God of the Hebrew people – alongside the other deities of the kingdom. In this case, the exclusivist approach of Daniel provided the missional opportunity for the Hebrew God to be worshipped by the people, albeit in a syncretistic fashion.

The book of Daniel then turns from being about a group of friends who gained political influence and yet remained faithful to the Hebrew God to being about how the God of the Hebrews remains faithful to God's chosen people in the experience of exile and beyond. Hope in the God of the Hebrews leads to an end-of-days vision of hope for the entire world.

Daniel embodies the cost and hope of what it means to maintain one's life of worship when the cultural and political powers of the day are set against such spiritual activities. Daniel and his friends were faithful in service and yet defiant in their rejection of politico-cultural decisions that impacted their daily worship. This exclusivist approach eventually meant that the Hebrew God became a significant feature of Babylonian, Persian and Greek cultural expression. These Hebrews were something of an anomaly, but there was something mightier than magic tricks at work here. Daniel is a book offering hope through strict resistance to the prevailing culture.

One of the most life-transforming experiences of my faith journey to date has been the opportunity to serve with a 24/7 prayer team on the party island of Ibiza. During the summer season, Ibiza becomes a place of pilgrimage for thousands, all drawn to the pulse of dance music, cheap alcohol, liberal attitudes to sex and a thriving drugs culture. At its best, Ibiza is a beautiful Balearic island, with gorgeous sunsets, white sandy beaches and a deep Spanish history. As we discovered on mission, there is also a dangerous undertone of hedonism, excess and abuse. The nights were spent escorting drunk teenagers home, seeking medical help for those in need, mopping up vomit in club toilets and building relationships with the workers on the island. As a team, we all agreed that we would not drink alcohol during our time on the island. With clubs called Eden, Paradise and Angel, the stuff of spirituality was not hard to uncover – but we needed to focus on our own discipleship as a team, so that we could engage with tourists and workers in their stress, distress and excess.

Christian hope can come through remaining pure and unpolluted from the current situation. An exclusivist approach focuses on remaining faithful to our Christian identity, despite the temptations and alternative opportunities all around us.

Assimilation

The book of Jeremiah offers a complimentary yet nuanced approach to hope in the midst of exile. Whereas Daniel sought to remain pure and 'undefiled' by Babylonian and Persian ways, Jeremiah encouraged a grieving people to engage with the new cultural and political landscape and to begin to reassess the Hebrew world view in response to the world and cultures around them. Rather than resist the culture, as Daniel did, Jeremiah encouraged a change of mindset and practice. He encouraged the people to get involved with the life they were now experiencing, to be less fearful of difference and to not be afraid of what was to come. For Jeremiah, living hope came through the participation of building a community. This was both a physical rebuilding as well as a reinterpretation of rituals, rites and doctrine in light of present experience.

Jeremiah was a reluctant prophet, fearing himself to be too young to be of any use to God. However, God called Jeremiah to 'say whatever I command you' (1:7), and thus began a ministry that started with prophesying the downfall of the remaining Jewish kingdom (which landed Jeremiah in prison) and culminated with encouraging God's people to thrive in the midst of the pain of exile. Crucially, Jeremiah never downplayed the pain and trauma of exile. Hope is not a prescription or vaccine against fear and despair; it is the willingness to discover life and love within these experiences.

Jeremiah's message of cultural assimilation in exile – a sort of 'get on with life and get involved' message – came from a place of great isolation, depression and loneliness. Jeremiah saw the pain of God's people and felt it deeply himself. He spent much of his early ministry telling the Hebrew people to get their house in order, to turn back to God and to prevent their desolation. His final revelations about the restoration of God's people through God's purposes of the exile were spoken from his own experience of great sadness and loss. For Jeremiah, his message of hope came from within the experience of vulnerability and tragedy, both for the Hebrew nation and for himself.

Jeremiah's message of hope to a grieving people is outlined in chapter 29, in a letter addressed to the people who had been adversely impacted by the reign of King Nebuchadnezzar:

> This is what the Lord Almighty, the God of Israel, says to all those I carried into exile from Jerusalem to Babylon: 'Build houses and settle down; plant gardens and eat what they produce. Marry and have sons and daughters; find wives for your sons and give your daughters in marriage, so that they too may have sons and daughters. Increase in number there; do not decrease. Also, seek the peace and prosperity of the city to which I have carried you into exile. Pray to the Lord for it, because if it prospers, you too will prosper.' Yes, this is what the Lord Almighty, the God of Israel, says: 'Do not let the prophets and diviners among you deceive you. Do not listen to the dreams you encourage them to have. They are prophesying lies to you in my name. I have not sent them,' declares the Lord.
>
> This is what the Lord says: 'When seventy years are completed for Babylon, I will come to you and fulfil my good promise to bring you back to this place. *For I know the plans I have for you,' declares the Lord, 'plans to prosper you and not to harm you, plans to give you hope and a future.* Then you will call on me and come and pray to me, and I will listen to you. You will seek me and find me when you seek me with all your heart. I will be found by you,' declares the Lord, 'and will bring you back from captivity. I will gather you from all the nations and places where I have banished you,' declares the Lord, 'and will bring you back to the place from which I carried you into exile.'
> JEREMIAH 29:4–14 (italics added)

Jeremiah called the people to account, but encouraged them to get involved with the empire around them – to build, to marry, to feast together. In turn, the prosperity of the prevailing culture would be the vehicle of the redemption of the Hebrew people. Hope was to be found in the act of engagement with an unknown environment (both geographic as well as social). From the pain of lament, where the people were having to remember their ancient songs in a strange land (Psalm 137:4), Jeremiah began to tune the people back into the ancient story of God's plans and purposes throughout the whole of creation. This passage, often used as a phrase of prayerful encouragement amid trial or transition, is in fact a statement of protest and promise in the midst of an anxiety-ridden, disgraced people. It speaks of discovering that God is active within, not separate from, this new experience. God's plans and purposes are not limited to those within the Jewish system; they are being worked out in places where traditionally God was assumed to be absent. This is significantly countercultural.

When we are challenged with such painful exilic experiences, we learn from Jeremiah that it can be through times of great pain, anguish and vulnerability that God is discovered in surprising ways. Hope is not something to be discovered *despite* our experience, but within it and through it. Hope does not mean that we avoid pain and trauma and homesickness. Hope means that we meet God in the midst of these challenging circumstances. Assimilation in the metaphorical experience of exile may cost us everything we once knew, but through it we discover the unchangeable character of God who is full of compassion, mercy, grace and love.

As Jeremiah reflects in the powerful and distressing poetry of Lamentations:

> I remember my affliction and my wandering,
>   the bitterness and the gall.
> I well remember them,
>   and my soul is downcast within me.

Yet this I call to mind
    and therefore I have hope:
Because of the Lord's great love we are not consumed,
    for his compassions never fail.
They are new every morning;
    great is your faithfulness.
LAMENTATIONS 3:19–23

Even when everything seems to be turning to dust around us, there is still the choice to have hope in God's compassion and to notice something of blessing amid exile-like turmoil.

One weekend my church organised an outing for our local church families. We went to a soft-play centre that was designed for adults and children alike. There were ball pits, rope swings, climbing apparatus and slides, all in garish primary colours, like a psychedelic army assault course. One piece of apparatus was a giant, totally vertical wooden slide. It was high – stomach-churningly, adrenaline-pumpingly high. The children there were completely fearless, throwing themselves off the edge and into the ether. My colleague and I were a little more cautious. We sat at the top of the slide for a very long time, weighing up our options and figuring that dropping several feet in the air was neither a dignified nor an enjoyable idea. Eventually, bored with our nerves and our lack of courage, one child screamed from the bottom of the slide, 'Prove your worth as our minister and just get on with it!' Such a challenge to my ego could not go unnoticed. I shut my eyes, took a deep breath, said a naive 'please let this be okay' sort of prayer and leapt off my perch.

Hope, joy and the defeat of fear can come through letting go, stepping out into the unknown and joining in with what is happening around us. Hope can be about jumping off the ledge, and facing the adrenalin rush with courage and bravery. Christian hope can involve discovering more about ourselves and about God in the midst of a new place and experience – an assimilation into a new understanding of presence, practice and possibility.

Vision

The book of Isaiah offers a slightly more nuanced world view than this assimilation project. Isaiah's prophetic words sought to challenge the Hebrew people to trust that even their current experience was not the last experience. There was still hope. God was still in control. The worst thing is never the last thing when God is involved. Isaiah went to great lengths to offer a reality check to the homesick Hebrew people, recognising the trauma of their situation and responding in a deeply pastoral manner so that they might be able to adventure into a new and dangerous place that was deeply alien and unsettling.

Ultimately, Isaiah offered a vision where another world was not only possible but was also in God's design and plan. Even the trauma of their situation would be overcome – and there was one coming to whom even worse would happen. Through this saviour, a whole new kingdom would come into existence. Isaiah invited the Hebrew people to imagine what a new world order would look like, pointing to the 'suffering servant' who would bring that into fruition. The process of prophetic imagination led to the fulfilment of God's promise to forge a new cultural identity, with all the possibilities of new behaviours, practices and attitudes, in which the community were invited to participate. Another world was possible, but it wasn't quite the world they had hoped for. The hope of the future lay in the promises of a God who called the people to a renewed sense of who God was.

Hopeful resistance required attentiveness to God's continuing work of salvation in whatever context the people found themselves.

Much of Isaiah's recasting of the future is found in chapters 40—55. These chapters offer a poetic view of God's participation in, and care for, the world. For the people, the exilic experience was often characterised by God's absence and lack of interest in the woes and pain of the people. The exile was experienced as a punishment for disobedience, rather than an invitation to new opportunities.

However, even as the bearer of divine justice, God is not vindictive and uncaring. God called on Isaiah to speak 'comfort' (40:1) to the people. Isaiah was to 'speak tenderly to Jerusalem' (40:2). It is notable that the promise of a future alternative reality was fuelled by compassion. Hope, for the people Isaiah was speaking to, was not salvation through annihilation. Instead, Isaiah spoke words of tenderness and concern, which mirrored the character of the God who was pastorally and compassionately invested in the situation. God was gentle towards those who were homesick, marginalised, excommunicated and frightened. In turn, these words of hope were not broadcast in advertising slogans or shouted from the street corners to anyone who might listen. Instead, Isaiah's hope and good news were whispered, as though they were communicated to the ears of lovers or in the quiet touch of friends. To the people:

> He gives strength to the weary
>> And increases the power of the weak.
> Even youths grow tired and weary,
>> And young men stumble and fall;
> But those who hope in the Lord
>> Will renew their strength.
>
> ISAIAH 40:29–31

A vision of hope came through tenderness – but also in the midst of pain and trauma, not despite it.

Hope is not a vaccine that eradicates all possibility of fear, despair, illness or disease. Hopeful resistance looks to the kingdom of God as a means of human flourishing and well-being within these experiences. God was not untouched by the pain of exile. Rather, the context of the exile induced God's promised vision for a new world to come to birth. It is all too easy to assume that God remained independent from creation – a passive person in the sky – rather than an engaged force of (re)creativity. However, Isaiah's words to the people showed that God was as distressed by the situation as they were. There was something new being brought to birth, and with that new potential came both great anguish and great joy. God births (some might say midwifes) this new reality into being, bringing new life to full flourishing. As Isaiah says, 'But now, like a woman in childbirth, I cry out, I gasp and pant' (42:14b).

Crucially in these chapters from Isaiah, God challenged the people to see that the vision for another world view to come was not limited by what they had known before. The new hope was not to be constrained by the political success of the past, nor was it to be defined by worship styles or belief systems. God called the people to notice that a new hope was to be found within and because of the systems of the day – not despite them. The future would be different. It wouldn't look like what was expected or happen in the way that the Hebrew people imagined their salvation and their saviour would look like. But there was still hope.

Hope is to be found in unexpected places and in the power of unexpected people. Jeremiah speaks to us of finding hope amid pain and despair. Daniel speaks of hope through standing against rulers and powers. Esther subverts the systems in order to influence powerholders. Hope in a new vision for the coming kingdom of God, according to Isaiah, will come not in the expected ways of power and prestige. The new kingdom will be one of peace, liberation and righteousness. It will come at a cost.

A new vision of hope does not rely on the present order of things staying the same. It is not a resignation to the status quo. Instead, hope is an active engagement with the promise that salvation is coming. God's plans and purposes may not always come in the ways they are expected or anticipated to be carried out, but another world is possible. Hope, in Isaiah's vision, came with a cost and with a dangerous paradox. The new kingdom would be a place where:

> The wolf will live with the lamb,
>   the leopard will lie down with the goat,
> the calf and the lion and the yearling together...

> and the lion will eat straw like the ox.
> The infant will play near the cobra's den,
>   and the young child will put its hand into the viper's nest.
> They will neither harm nor destroy.
>
> ISAIAH 11:6–9

According to Isaiah, hopeful resistance is revolutionary and costly. Another world is possible, and it is God's work to enable it, even midwife it, into fruition. New possibilities are brought to birth by a re-creative God of resurrection and restoration, from within the contexts, experiences and cultures in which God's people find themselves. A vision for the present as well as the future is fertile ground for hope; but it's a hope that is full of surprises. The future doesn't look like what we might expect, but this is not something to fear. It is something to work towards and engage with. Hope for a new future means striving for ways to show that God's purposes are bigger and brighter than any present-day conflict or scheme.

It was a Thursday afternoon. A peaceful protest against increases in student fees had attracted tens of thousands of marchers to Westminster. As the march progressed, a dissident few began to turn the march into a riot. People were kettled by police, and large pockets of protesters became violent. I was due to lead worship at Central Hall Westminster – a stone's throw from parliament (pun, in this instance, intended). Despite road restrictions and underground train closures, I managed to make my way through the back streets of Westminster and eventually talked my way through the cordon. I was escorted by the local constabulary through the rioting students to the door of the church. As the rioting reached its pinnacle outside the building, I lifted bread and wine before a small gathering of brave congregants, and began to say the words of institution at Communion: 'This is my body, broken for you.' It was a precious moment of hope amid chaos. Surrounded by violence, kettled within a military-style cordon, in a security lockdown situation, the gospel was embodied and re-enacted. Together we maintained a community of worshippers who celebrated a vision of the salvation of the world, through the broken and bruised body of Jesus, shrouded in the midst of broken bottles, bruised students and bloodied police officers.

Hope clings on to the vision that another world is possible, even if it comes at a cost.

So what?

Subversion, exclusivism, assimilation and vision are all valid responses to the experience of exile. They offer a range of insights into the nature of God and into God's relationship with the Hebrew people. They are not mutually exclusive, but they do invite participation, prophetic imagination and pastoral sensitivity. Crucially, none of these responses are passive. Ignorance is not an option. Deep within the experience of exile is the invitation to discover more about the creator God and God's purposes for humanity. Despite the people's feeling as though God is absent and wallowing in the misunderstanding that exile is a punishment for disobedience, in each of these four options lies the opportunity to step up, move forwards, engage in discipleship and discover more about God in the midst of a believing community.

To live hopefully, we need to be proactive, participatory, prophetic.

By taking Brueggemann's metaphorical approach seriously, these avenues of response and relationship are also open to us during our troubling and anxious times. Hopeful resistance gives us options and actions. There are structures to challenge, and there are systems to engage with. There are invitations to celebrate, and there are experiences to wrestle with. The model of exile means that there is a blueprint for not only surviving our current situation but also thriving within it. The exile provides the space to deepen our spirituality. There is the invitation to build new relationships with strange people. There is the call to authentic living, which means that hurt, fear, pain and tragedy become part of our story rather than things to be avoided. Ultimately, the metaphor of exile enables us to journey towards God: the compassionate, loving, merciful, re-creative one who acts for, not against, God's people.

At the point in human experience when life becomes unbearable and our questions become too bold and painful, God speaks and offers hope and a renewed future for the believing community. A God-centred theology of hope brings us face-to-face with the God of restoration and re-creation, who can be found in the midst of, not despite, the doubt and the pain.

It's easy to hope that things will get better, but when everything seems to be out of control, fear can override all sense of hope. Yet God is a God of hopeful living and compassionate grace. God's character of love, peace, mercy, justice, righteousness, graciousness and compassion has the power and the expectation to overcome the guilt, shame, terror and fear of this moment.

Within the metaphor of the exile – whether we take a subversive, exclusivist, assimilative or visionary approach – there remain practical examples of living hopefully.

1 *Keep worshipping.* Whether it is penning poetry, singing the songs of the ancient land or discovering new ways to worship God, it is through worship that God's people will find hope in a culture of fear.

2 *Build relationships, not barriers.* Hope comes through taking the risk of authentic and honest relationships. It is in faithful communities of people that the embrace of God continues to cast itself wider and wider.

3 *Tell it like it is.* Tell your story. Don't sugar-coat it. Lament if you need to (it's why the psalms are so important). Laugh if you

can. Acknowledge anger and pain, especially in those situations that shake our understanding and leave us in an unexpected or hostile place. Share your stories of hope and hopelessness with those who live and love alongside you. The pastor and theologian Diana Butler Bass suggests that by telling our personal stories, sharing the intimate and difficult parts of life together, 'there is a profound honesty of authentic community, a rare awareness of God's presence in the mundane, and a palpable sense of hope'. Personal, honest stories, dripping with integrity and informality, coupled with the use of imagery and poetry and the creative arts, have the power to change the world.

4 *Pay attention to what God is doing.* Get involved if you can. Simple things like taking note of the changing seasons, going for a walk, eating slowly and sitting still can all help to realign our breathing, thinking, feeling and sensitivity to the present moment. In turn, listening, asking questions, staying inquisitive and learning to disagree well with other people can help to shape our sensitivity to the marks of God's grace in our lives. Hope often dwells on the edges of our experience and existence. We need to find ways to notice these margins and to push ourselves outwards.

In an age of great complexity and with a fear of the unknown, hope pushes towards the unknown rather than away from it. One way to live with hope and to challenge the power of despair and hopelessness is to be open to the very things we are afraid of. In the midst of humanity's hopelessness and despair, God is the steadying force and source that enables life to continue to be worth living – in the present as well as for the future.

God's presence is not limited to the realm of the religious. We learn throughout scripture that God is present in the alien context as well as, and often despite, the religious. God is always seeking to expand the kingdom among those whom the world marginalises and persecutes. What marks Christian hope in dangerous, even exilic, times? The community of believers who begin to intentionally reflect

God's character. How do we live hopefully in threatening times? We become a community of mercy, love, justice, compassion, peace and grace. How do we enable our families to thrive amid fear? We become a home characterised by mercy, love, justice, compassion, peace and grace. Why? Because we know the power of the God who is revealed throughout terror, trauma and travail as a God of mercy, love, justice, compassion, peace and grace.

In the midst of exile, when everything that is known is falling to dust, when the surroundings are strange and relationships are strained, in the courage of remaining faithful to God, God remains faithful to the people, revealing to them the characteristics shown to their forebears. Hope is found in the creator God, whose love is demonstrated in compassion, grace, justice and peace.

Hopelessness, despair and fear leave us stranded, agnostic and ambivalent. We become homesick for another age and another place, and we become passive, cynical and spiritually dry. Hope, however, says that another world is possible. Our alternative is to seek God and to participate in the kingdom at work. We are to engage with the world we are in, through subversion, exclusivism, assimilation or vision. As we engage, we discover, and in turn offer, hope – through worship, relationships, storytelling and attentiveness. Through these prophetic actions and routine rituals, we may just begin to see God's promises at work for the good of all people.

The whisper comes.

Another world is possible.

Questions for reflection

- When have you felt homesick? How did it feel to return home again?

- In what ways does exile as a metaphor help us to understand our current situation and a hope-filled way of living?

- When have you been subversive, exclusive, assimilative, and/or visionary?

- What do you notice about the character of God in the discussion in this chapter?

- What might God be birthing in your local/national context, and who are the people God is using to achieve these purposes? What is your response to this?

4

Gardener's world

I heard a loud voice from the throne saying, 'Look! God's dwelling-place is now among the people, and he will dwell with them. They will be his people, and God himself will be with them and be their God. "He will wipe every tear from their eyes. There will be no more death" or mourning or crying or pain, for the old order of things has passed away.'

REVELATION 21:3–4

Hope's home is at the innermost point in us, and in all things. It is a quality of aliveness. It does not come at the end, as the feeling that results from a happy outcome. Rather, it lies at the beginning, as a pulse of trust that sends us forth. When our innermost being is attuned to this pulse it will send us forth in hope, regardless of the physical circumstances of our lives. Hope fills us with the strength to stay present.

Cynthia Bourgeault, *Mystical Hope* (Cowley, 2001)

The northern lights

Visiting Iceland had been on our bucket list for a while. There was something compelling about the possibility of seeing the northern lights, visiting the world's largest greenhouse-propagated tomato plantation and eating warm cinnamon buns, in one short stay among the icefields and glaciers. It also happened to be my husband's Big Birthday, so I hatched a cunning plan. With thermals packed, we set out on what was to become our babymoon/birthday celebration minibreak.

Iceland is a fascinating, otherworldly place. It is a country used by sci-fi filmmakers, due to the stark geology of lava rock formations and glaciers, making it inhospitable outside of the main conurbations. Yet there is something beautiful about a country that has been formed and reshaped not only through political alliances, but also, and mainly, through geographic and geological turbulence over millennia. The Icelandic landscape is always in flux, ever changing due to an incoming ice storm or a volcanic eruption or through the changes caused by geothermal activity just beneath the surface.

On our arrival, we were advised to prebook the evening's tour to see the northern lights. It turns out the conditions required to produce the aurora are rather fickle and unreliable, and so we heeded the advice.

Our coach tour picked us up at the appointed hour and took us to the place where meteorologists had determined we had the best chance of seeing the phenomena. Coach after coach rolled into the same small car park on the coastal edge of Iceland, as tour operators took advantage of the day's promise of a spectacle, based in this particular coastal location. In turn, the coaches belched out the tourist congregation, as hundreds of cold foreigners, all snuggled in layer upon layer of clothing, headed out on to the headland to stare at the stars.

It was freezing: −15 Celsius according to the thermometer gauge in the coach. Out on the headland, the wind blowing in from the Atlantic Ocean made it feel even colder. The only soundtrack for the evening was the deafening blow of the wind, the sound of teeth chattering and the roar of the sea as it crashed against the cliff face beneath us. It was certainly atmospheric.

We waited, staring into the cloudy abyss of the night. We waited for the telltale shimmer of silver, sweeping high above us. We waited for the famous green luminescence to dance across the sky. We waited until our fingers and toes froze, and we were forced to retreat back into the warmth of the coach. We waited for what we knew was there, but never quite appeared.

We have photos of strange blobs in the sky, obscured by the clouds, but still eerily promising that the night's performance was in full flow – just not so that we could see it. We caught glimpses of the silver shimmer, but only insofar as it looked like the clouds really did have a silver lining.

We waited, but we were never blessed with a full demonstration of what had been promised in all the pamphlets and pictures of life in Iceland. We waited for three more days, but the lights failed to perform for our visit.

Our Iceland experience parallels something of the paradox of resurrection hope – that tension which recognises that there is both a present and a future reality to be experienced. We catch glimpses of the present transformation of hope, as poverty is challenged and when people are healed. But it is also somehow strangely not quite here yet. What marks resurrection hope out as exceptional and different from any emotionally driven pseudo-psychology is that it is a hope which promises something for a future yet unknown.

In Iceland, we knew something was there. Something was happening. But we couldn't quite see it properly. As Paul says to the Corinthians, 'For now we see through a glass, darkly; but then face to face: now I know in part; but then shall I know even as also I am known' (1 Corinthians 13:12, KJV).

This chapter is about those things that we know are there but can't grasp entirely: life after death and our responsibility of life before death. The academic word for this know-it-but-can't-see-it-yet experience is 'eschatology'. It reflects back on a past paradise, lost to humanity. It also looks to the resurrection hope offered through Jesus and to a kingdom that is breaking into our present reality. It has a future dimension, which calls into place a future hope for the whole of creation. To help us engage with these tensions, this chapter relies on a number of visual cameos: the northern lights, a series of gardens and an art installation. Each of these events serve to shift our hopeful gaze from an end-of-life insurance policy to an openness to living Christian hope each and every day.

The first movement in finding God in a culture of fear is to discover Christian hope for oneself: to discover the life-bringing nature of the kingdom of God in the ministry of Jesus, the promise of the resurrection and the inspiration of the Holy Spirit. From discovering hope in our midst, discipleship is then about unearthing and birthing this hope for other people and the whole of creation.

This chapter sets out a threefold movement or flow of eschatology, grounded in an ecological model of future hope, intentionally contrasting with some of the more familiar models of economic processes of justice and atonement. As with our star-gazing in Iceland, there is something out there and other, yet it is also profoundly present in our contemporary setting, and it is confirmed by all that we know of the past. Christian hope and faithful hopeful resistance to a culture of fear are organic processes.

Sewage works to spiritual haven: an ecology of eschatology

In the corner pocket of a South Yorkshire village lay the remnants of the old sewage works. The council were selling off the land cheaply, and it was eventually purchased by a Christian couple looking for a final pre-retirement project. This unpromising piece of land, at the end of a narrow and bumpy bridleway, became their oasis. Where others merely saw the sewage works, this couple saw rich soil, divided plots and the opportunity for hope and healing to be offered to all. Over the course of five years, they transformed the weed fields and crumbling concrete of dereliction into a public garden and tearoom.

The garden itself became a place for people living with educational needs to be apprenticed in gardening skills, where they were accepted as volunteers and then trained and resourced as gardeners. The café began to offer volunteer jobs to people living with depression. It was a place of solace where people could provide tea and cake for visitors, but only have to engage with people as they wanted to, a practice of routine and simplicity that gave people a reason to leave the house for an hour – or ten minutes if that day was particularly bleak. They served the best lemon meringue pie I have ever tasted (the recipe remains a closely guarded secret). The garden landscape itself began to be a place of consolation and healing for visitors – many of whom used the pathways and the multisensory nature of the garden for their own therapeutic purposes. The garden changed with the seasons and became a community space so popular with local residents that the council eventually bought the entire plot back, having also invested in additional infrastructure: a car park, toilet facilities (ironically) and a tarmacked road.

The garden also hosted marriage proposals, engagement parties, weddings and the scattering of ashes, as it gained a reputation as a safe and sacred space for the most important and transitional times in people's lives. The local church began to invest as both volunteers and chaplains, holding open harvest festival celebrations with the local allotment owners (who themselves toiled the plot of land next door). There were solstice songs of praise evenings and healing ministry offered outside of normal operating hours. The tearoom became a listening space, where people could talk freely and openly about the things of life. At the heart of the garden remained a faithful Christian couple and their small group of prayerful friends, who saw the potential of both a medical necessity and a derelict part of town.

There is something profoundly gospel about this story. It's a narrative of hope that comes out of the most disgusting and desolate of spaces. It opens the potential of the organic nature of the kingdom of God. Furthermore, it is an ongoing example of the power of gardens in the gospel. Throughout scripture, gardens host the gospel. Gardens provide the backdrop and the setting into which God acts and through which resurrection hope flourishes. The whole of salvation history takes place within a series of gardens.

Garden one: Eden

In the beginning, the perfect place was created for humanity to dwell and reside with God. It was a place of stewardship, where human beings were able to collaborate with nature and where the relationship with God was tangible and playful. There was only one rule – not to eat the fruit of the tree of the knowledge of good and evil. Human beings were inquisitive and, egged on by another creature, a serpent, disobeyed God and, in turn, lost paradise.

Eden was the place of everything and became the place of nothing. It was a place of presence and became the place of absence.

All it took was a forbidden fruit from a forbidden tree. It sounds like the opening of a fairy story rather than the opening sequence of the creation poem of scripture. A single commandment from God was broken by the very people who should have known better.

The dislocation of relationships in Genesis 3 was catastrophic, following the fruity ingestion. First, humans became aware of their bodies and were body-shamed into covering up. This became a feature of God's compassion in response to their disobedience, however, as 'God made garments of skin for Adam and his wife' (v. 21). God the fashion designer, even in the midst of anger and betrayal, served humanity and provided for them. God continues to act with tenderness and compassion towards humanity, despite humanity's flagrant transgression.

Second, there was a strange game of hide-and-seek, as Adam and Eve attempted for the first time to hide from God – alert perhaps to God's sense of justice and anger at their disobedience. Then, Adam and Eve played the blame game; neither took responsibility for the fall, but both were intent on finding someone else to take the credit/ blame.

Finally, there was a swift proclamation of God's justice, as the serpent and the humans received their punishment – a final fracturing of relationship between God and humans, between humans and the wider creation, and indeed between God and creation.

At every turn, there is carnage and pain. Relationships crack, and there is no way back from the holy perfection of the first garden. There is very little hope.

In his book *Ladies and Gentlemen, the Bible!* (Riverhead Books, 2009), Jonathan Goldstein rewrites Bible stories for a contemporary audience. His version of the creation story ends with this powerful narrative of lost hope and shame:

> During the darkest days ahead, with the fratricides and whatnot, Adam would often think back to his brief time in Eden. As he became an old man, he would talk about the garden more and more. A couple of times he had even tried to find his way back there, but he very soon became lost. He didn't try too hard anyway. He didn't want to bother God any more than he already had. When Adam met someone that he really liked, he would say, I so wish you could have been there. It didn't seem fair to him that he was the one that got to be in Eden.

> This sunset isn't bad, he'd say. But the sunsets in Eden, they burned your nose hairs. They made your ears bleed. He couldn't even explain it right. When you ate the fruit in Eden it was like eating God, he would say. And God was delicious. When you wanted him you just grabbed him. Now when he ate fruit he can only taste what was not there.

The newly exiled humans enter a new experience – one where sin and disobedience continue to evolve. The biblical accounts following the exit from Eden see intrigue and murder within this first family, leading eventually to God's decision to annihilate the whole of the created order from the earth – a sort of control-alt-delete restart on the whole experiment.

Hope is not destruction; it is participation in cultivating something new.

From this point on, God continued to be in the business of reconciliation and restoration – and the rest of biblical history speaks about a God who wants to put the relationships between human, creation and the divine back on track. Eschatology imagines how God will achieve this ultimate aim of bringing humanity back to Eden.

The hopeful resistance, putting the pieces back together, has begun, and it all began in a garden.

Garden two: Jesus' death and resurrection

Jesus was arrested in the garden of Gethsemane, executed on Jerusalem's rubbish heap and buried in the borrowed garden tomb of Joseph of Arimathea, a well-respected Jewish leader and intrigued (if not fully fledged) Jesus-follower. Once again, gardens played host to the outworking of God's plan and purpose, as Jesus willingly chose the cost of crucifixion in order that paradise and relationship be restored to God's people.

Even the thief crucified with Jesus was promised 'Today you will be with me in paradise' (Luke 23:43). This was a controversial political statement of intent – a statement of overthrowing the Roman rulers of the day. It was also a theological declaration, inviting a final, broken, searching sinner the opportunity to discover hope in the grace of God.

There's hope for all. Paradise remains open to anyone who seeks it out, saint or sinner, celebrity or thief. God has always been, and still is, in the business of cultivation and (re)creation. Through Jesus, there is hope that the present (whenever that is) is not the end of anybody's story – as Mary found out.

Standing at the entrance to a garden owned by Joseph of Arimathea, the garden took centre stage – as Mary mistook the resurrected Jesus for the gardener. There are many reasons why Mary should have missed this particular moment. Her world had fallen apart. In her brokenness, she had no sense of hope or everything being fixed. She made a bold choice of words and jumped to a simple assumption – a person in the garden must be the gardener. What she, and we, may have missed is that Jesus had already made the connection between resurrection hope and the garden: 'I am the true vine, and my Father is the gardener' (John 15:1). Mary, full of fear and out of hope, met this gardener God face-to-face.

In this garden, with the borrowed tomb mirroring the borrowed stable of his birth, Jesus demonstrated that the ultimate hope is to be found in the resurrection, and that this re-creative order is not only for broken humanity but also for the whole of creation. The gardener is tending to humanity once again. The relationships lost at Eden was redeemed and restored. The gardener, God, is cultivating a new world order. Atonement, salvation, restoration and love are forged not in a debating chamber but in dirt and loam.

As the case of mistaken identity unfolded, the power of the resurrection garden becomes apparent. This garden hosted the most powerful of experiences and expressions of the kingdom of God: Jesus is alive. Restitution is made. Love wins. The promises lost in Eden have been restored.

Despite having spent several years in his company, Mary, when faced with the 'gardener', failed to recognise who was standing in front of her. There are many ways in which this passage has been used to diminish Mary's participation in this story and to demean her honest engagement. For some, this is further evidence against female sensibility in the midst of chaos. It has been suggested that Jesus was somehow distorted in her vision through her tears. It's possible that Jesus' physical appearance still bore the marks of his trial, so Mary was just confused by the horror of bruises and dishevelment. Mary has thus become caricatured as emotionally unstable or suffering from post-traumatic stress following the brutality of the crucifixion she had witnessed days previously.

But what if there is an alternative to this view? What if John is really trying to suggest that, post-resurrection, things look different to the way they did before? That there was actually something different about Jesus' appearance that affected the unravelling of the whole scene?

Turn around. See things differently.

The worst thing seemed like the last thing, but it didn't stop Mary from engaging and participating in the life and world she now experienced. Even when the future had no meaning, when everything appeared futile, there was a pull, a draw, towards a different reality. Another world was possible – even if it was a future filled with the aroma of spices over a friend's body. Mary, the woman who stayed when the rest of Jesus' friends fled into the darkness just a few days prior. Mary, the woman who arrived with spices to bless her friend. Mary, the woman who faced the real possibility of her own arrest, as she entered the garden, rather than staying behind in the safety of a locked room. Mary, who ran towards Jesus, despite religious conventions that prohibited her from doing so. Mary, the truth teller. Mary, who learnt the power of turning around.

As she did so, she discovered the ultimate truth. At the heart of the gospel is the hope that the worst thing is never the last thing. Turn around, and see things differently.

Her name was whispered on his lips: 'Mary,' said the gardener/ stranger/Jesus. In that moment, the whole of human life and experience would never be the same again, for Mary or for the rest of the world.

The heart of grace, found in the gospel, is the hope that death is never the end of the story. Resurrection hope is not a promise that humanity is to evade death and decay; such experiences are a given. However, what this garden encounter between Mary and the gardener/Jesus demonstrates is that life looks different from the other side of death. We should not evade the visceral or physical nature of transition times. There is something other, something different, that occurs on the other side of death, which cannot be described or contemplated – but which is experienced by those who are courageous and who press into the deeper, richer story as it unfolds.

It's not an easy story, but as Mary shows, it's well worth the wait.

It is easy to forget that the garden sequence of the crucifixion and resurrection saw Jesus choose to take a path that would lead to his death, and then offer life beyond death to those who were at the lowest point in their life. The once-Jewish community no longer experienced life as full of despair, anxiety and trauma. The friends were able to speak Jesus' name and to discover afresh what life after death was all about.

An ecology of atonement and eschatology means that there is always the option to cultivate a new reality, although it is a choice not without pain or challenge. Choosing to die in order for life to flourish is a powerful theological statement. It is at the heart of the gospel: 'Greater love has no one than this: to lay down one's life for one's friends' (John 15:13). It is shocking, therefore, that from the time of the first disciples to the present day, communities prefer a palliative approach to mission and ministry in order to stave off the inevitability of decline and irrelevance, rather than trusting and hoping in the promise of resurrection. The disciples huddled together in hiding, until Mary's screams broke their silence. Thomas missed out and, in his obstinacy, refused to believe the stories – wanting to see and touch this new kingdom world for himself. Judas didn't wait for his restorative re-engagement with the risen Jesus, calling time on his participation in the story. Time and time again, the resurrection promise of hope and life in all its fullness is thwarted and resisted by the very people who should know better. In chapels and in projects, we strive and struggle to remain alive, resuscitating projects and congregations well beyond their lifespan, because even a glimpse of resurrection hope and 'what happens next' is terrifying. It won't look like it did before.

But then, neither did Jesus.

Garden three: Eden restored in the garden city

John's promise and vision in Revelation 21—22 speak about this final garden where the relationship between God and humanity is ultimately restored, where hope is finally realised. Christian hope is about the ultimate destination of humanity – the final garden city. This is where despair has no power, where tears are replaced with praise, where God once again freely walks among the created order and where humanity works and rests by the rivers of healing.

This is a pastorally rich and vibrant promise – one which restores God's relationship to humanity and which in turn restores humanity's relationship with creation. There is no shame, guilt, fear or despair. This is a place where hope is transformed into reality and where there is healing and wholeness for the whole created order.

God begins with a garden, in Eden, and at the end of time promises to restore hope and relationship in a garden city through Jesus' passion, in all things bringing together humanity in community and unity.

At the turn of the 20th century in the UK, there was a shift in the way housing developments were curated. Inspired by the desire to shape a community around the three tenets of residential, industrial and agricultural principles, urban planning began to focus on 'garden cities'. These were large conurbations on the outskirts of major cities, intentionally developed to promote healthy lifestyles, access to industry and green spaces for agriculture and pleasure. Inspired by the creative work of Sir Ebenezer Howard, designs of this kind have been transplanted around the world, both through the Commonwealth colonies and beyond. Although these garden cities did not evolve in precisely the way Howard envisaged, they still form part of the developments in urban areas and have also influenced the gentrification movements of suburban city planning.

Garden cities are not the sole purview of Howard and his funders, however. The ultimate garden city is that shared by John in Revelation. The end of all things will come with a garden city – a place of dwelling, rest, work and healing; arguably a place of residential, industrial and agricultural principles at work; a place of soulfulness as well as joyfulness.

At the end of the whole of scripture, in the final chapters of Revelation, comes God's vision for the end of all times. The book begins with a warning to the churches about their ambivalence and indifference to the political and theological reality around them. The middle part is full of apocalyptic visions and battles and metaphors that demonstrate the trials and tribulations of life before God's final consummation of creation in the holy garden city. The vision concludes with a description of what the promised paradise will look like. It will be a restoration of Eden but not a returning to Eden. Resurrection, after all, looks like something different.

The Holy City, Jerusalem, coming down out of heaven from God. It shone with the glory of God, and its brilliance was like that of a very precious jewel, like a jasper, clear as crystal. It had a great, high wall with twelve gates, and with twelve angels at the gates. On the gates were written the names of the twelve tribes of Israel. There were three gates on the east, three on the north, three on the south and three on the west. The wall of the city had twelve foundations, and on them were the names of the twelve apostles of the Lamb…

I did not see a temple in the city, because the Lord God Almighty and the Lamb are its temple. The city does not need the sun or the moon to shine on it, for the glory of God gives it light, and the Lamb is its lamp. The nations will walk by its light, and the kings of the earth will bring their splendour into it. On no day will its gates ever be shut, for there will be no night there. The glory and honour of the nations will be brought into it. Nothing impure will ever enter it, nor will anyone who does what is shameful or deceitful, but only those whose names are written in the Lamb's book of life.

Then the angel showed me the river of the water of life, as clear as crystal, flowing from the throne of God and of the Lamb down the middle of the great street of the city. On each side of the river stood the tree of life, bearing twelve crops of fruit, yielding its fruit every month. And the leaves of the tree are for the healing of the nations. No longer will there be any curse. The throne of God and of the Lamb will be in the city, and his servants will serve him. They will see his face, and his name will be on their foreheads. There will be no more night. They will not need the light of a lamp or the light of the sun, for the Lord God will give them light.

REVELATION 21:10–14; 21:22—22:5

Throughout Revelation, the challenge is given to the Christian church to step up and step into the promises of a new heaven and a new earth. This is a busy, bustling city full of people and work and song and hope and peace and joy and compassion. This is where God's character of love, courage, compassion and creativity are given full expression, and where there is a place for anyone who takes up the invitation through Jesus, for the gates are always open.

Rich in detail and dripping with metaphor, the vision of the holy garden city is marked also by what is *not* there:

1   There is no more sea – an ancient metaphor for chaos. In this holy city, the chaos and complexity have passed. All the questions and power-dealing have been silenced. There will be no more chaos; the waters of fear and despair have been quenched in the river of life.

2   There is no temple, because God resides with the people, without needing to be contained in a building. There is no designated place to worship, because the whole city is a space of worship alongside God; God is present in all things, not in a designated or specific location.

3   There is no need for light, and there is no sun and no moon. This means that the city is safe and secure, and it also indicates that God is stronger than other celestial deities given power and influence at the time of John's revelation. The battles have stopped. The exile is over.

4   There is no more death or mourning.

5   There is no more curse – a reference to the curse in Genesis 3.

In the city, there is room for everyone whose name appears in the book of life. Those within the walls are surrounded by beauty and hope. This is a place where hope is fulfilled and where people are reconciled to each other and to the created order.

With Adam's expulsion from Eden, there was a specific command not to return. Here, there is an open invitation to return:

> The Spirit and the bride say, 'Come!' And let the one who hears say, 'Come!' Let the one who is thirsty come; and let the one who wishes take the free gift of the water of life.
> REVELATION 22:17

The final promise of paradise is not like that which has been experienced before. This is a new paradigm that nurtures invitation and participation. The new heaven and new earth are places of dwelling with God in a way that is completely new. The river and tree of life are returned, as is humanity's place alongside them – but this is a new holy garden city, not merely Eden restored to its former glory.

There is an important 'not yet' dimension to eschatology – a future vision to which humanity is called to strive. There are glimpses of this yet-to-be kingdom in the present, just as there was a glimmer of the northern lights in our Iceland expedition; but resurrection hope requires us to wait and to watch, because what happens next isn't quite like anything we have seen before. An ecological approach to salvation, atonement and eschatology requires patience, cultivation, nurture and ongoing tending.

The gospel, the source of all 'hope-full-ness', can be told in gardens. Salvation history, resurrection hope and end-times theology are hosted in garden-based movements. A present/future community is cultivated in gardens: gardens that hold the story of the paradoxes of promise and loss, friendship and betrayal, hope and despair. All that is lost in Eden is redeemed in the resurrection encounters of Jesus, and then nurtured and supported into its final revelation and refashioning as the final garden city.

The gospel is the story of the gardener's world.

An ecology of eschatology (or gardens of grace) offers something of an alternative to the more economic models of salvation history. An ecology offers something organic, whereas the economic models are more transactional in approach. Traditionally, who and how people are saved has been framed by a crude form of assumed questions and argumentative apologetics, arguing people into submission based on a few universal longings rather than building up a relationship for the long haul:

1   If the world is full of sin and personal guilt, salvation requires an innocent to pay the price.

2   If at the heart of all things is an angry and vengeful deity who needs to be assuaged by some form of sacrificial offering, there needs to be an innocent victor and a bloody battleground at best, or the starkly controversial 'divine child abuse' at worst.

3   If there is a narrative of shame that overwhelms an entire community, good news must speak of corporate dignity and worth that moves beyond personal accountability and towards a holistic understanding of life-givingness.

4   If there is institutional corruption, salvation requires there to be a liberating and loving alternative to the political and industrial systems that oppress the weak and powerless.

However, a more organic, dirty, messy version of atonement theology, which grows within the cold frame of the garden sequences, means that the divine flow is the source of all hope, that Jesus is the model for our own discipleship and that ultimate hope is to be discovered in the everyday practice of gestures of grace and love. Just as seeds need to die in order to flourish, so hope needs to be planted and tended in order to grow – but as it does, it changes the whole of the world in its wake.

It's tempting to be so preoccupied with balancing the scales of justice that we miss the visceral, earthy, dirty-hands-and-feet nature of Jesus' ministry. Jesus was in an organic kingdom business. As we will see in the next chapter, Jesus served food – loaves and fish – to thousands, told stories about trees and vines and fields, hewed corn in his hands in order to prove a point and spoke about a farmer who sowed seed recklessly and abundantly. Jesus' methods were not economic; they were ecological. Thus the garden, and not the courtroom, hosts the gospel, and in turn offers the seeds of grace to our lives.

There has been a tendency in the last century to downplay the theological framework of creation, prioritising a theology of fall and redemption as some sort of eternal escape plan for a chosen, well-behaved few. It has led to the divorce of creation care from church life, the denial of creativity in places of worship and the exclusion of people who fail to conform to a set pattern of behaviours.

In the present day, life (both personal and corporate) is a paradox of brokenness and restoration, despair and hope, experienced by so many in Gethsemane and garden-tomb moments. Any sense of resurrection seems implausible, and humanity is left, like Mary, pondering where Jesus can be. Yet the garden sequences provide a narrative which says that God is still tending to humanity, cultivating a new world order that will be both a place of knowledge and a space of grace and healing. Hope is growing, grafted into our lives and blossoming when we need it the most.

The three gardens enable an investigation into the ecology of eschatology that reflects on the past, present and future realities of the coming kingdom of God.

So what? Turn around

In 2009, the large empty shell of the Turbine Hall in the Tate Modern in London hosted an exhibition by the Polish artist Mirosław Bałka. The exhibit, entitled 'How it is', was one of the first pieces of installation art to have graced the inside of the former power station. The installation itself, on first viewing at least, was a little more disappointing than its billing – a large shipping container, painted in shades of black. Its insides were coated in a soft foam, inevitably as a health-and-safety precaution but which also acted as a powerful soundproofing device.

To experience the installation, rather than observe it, one had to walk up a steep incline – a sort of ramp of doom – in order to enter the box. Each step towards the open side of the container was one further step into the darkness. Experiencing this piece of art makes you feel vulnerable. It is terrifying. And yet it is also somewhat exhilarating at the same time. People bustle and bump into each other, as participants in the artwork become desensitised to the darkness and yet totally blind to what is all around them. People sit alongside the walls; some people also use the walls for guidance, increasing the sense of jeopardy in the exhibit. Other people kneel or stand at the open side, trying to catch a glimpse of what is inside or pondering the invitation of the darkness – yet they are unable to step into the abyss. Children run and scream, the sound buffered by the container itself. Collisions are inevitable. Each and every participant at once is part of a community, and yet totally isolated and alone in their own experience of it.

Many things have been written about Bałka's box. Is it a metaphor for immigration – a more contemporary offering in a world now surrounded by images of human trafficking into eastern Europe? Or, from a Polish perspective, is it a social commentary on the Holocaust? For some it is a model of 21st-century living – an empty shell within which we are invited to exist until our end comes, and our final resting place is another, much smaller box: ashes to ashes, dust to dust. Or is it a safety shell, protecting us from others and the rest of the world? Is it a chance to become anonymous for a while or merely to sink into the abyss – a suicide of sorts?

There is something terrifying about the darkness, as it envelops and smothers anything in its path, destroying hope and parading despair in its wake. Perhaps this is the inheritance of horror movies, perpetuating the myth that all major devastation happens at night. Perhaps it is because the darkness also heightens our alertness and awareness of our other senses, as we rely less on what we can see and more on ethereal noises and strange sensations.

One of the most moving things about Bałka's box isn't to be found in the experience of continually stepping into the darkness – as profound an experience as that might be. The genius of this piece of art comes when you reach the very back of the container – 30 metres of walking which can feel like a mile. When you get to the very back – having stumbled and felt your way past other adventurers – that is not the end of the journey.

The darkness is never the end of the story. The worst thing is never the last thing. At what seems to be the very end of the darkness, there remains a single invitation. There is one further response, whispering in the darkness: 'Turn around.' The ancients might add, 'Repent!'

And as you turn around, you become overwhelmed by the power of the light facing you, for as you turn around, you are faced with the open side and the steep-sloped entranceway. You squint. You turn away. You cover your eyes. You are in many ways blinded by the grace of the experience of being totally lost, encompassed in your own story. In many ways it can lead to despair. However, the darkness, even in Bałka's installation, doesn't have the last word; it plays host to the next adventure – the adventure of light.

This dual experience – dark and light – mirrors that of the central gardens in the gospel – Gethsemane and the empty tomb. The eschatological conundrum of the kingdom of God is both now and not yet. Hope in our present circumstances needs the creative tension between these experiences in order to offer hope in the midst of despair. There needs to be both an engagement with the negative and a knowledge of the positive. Dark, Gethsemane, Not Yet only make sense when held alongside hope and trust in their opposites: Light, Tomb, Now.

The hope we have for the future consummation of the kingdom of God is not an anaesthetic to our current circumstances. It is the promise of an engaged and compassionate God, revealing the nature of grace and the inclusivity of the gospel. As Jürgen Moltmann suggests in *Theology of Hope* (SCM, 2010):

The knowledge of the future that is kindled by promise is therefore a knowledge in hope, is therefore prospective and anticipatory, but is therefore also provisional, fragmentary, open, straining beyond itself.

As we struggle with our contemporary experience, hoping beyond hope that another world is possible and living with the stories that prove time and again that the worst thing is never the last thing, there is, more than ever, a need to notice those glimpses of the kingdom of God at work in our midst: to turn around and be blinded by the light.

On earth as it is in heaven.

In yet another beautiful kingdom paradox, hope becomes most powerful at the point at which despair is named, recognised, embraced and battled through – the point where you reach the rear of Bałka's box, and the internal whisper encourages you to turn around and to embrace the whole of the experience of life.

Dark. Gethsemane. Not Yet.

Light. Tomb. Now.

The lights have been flicked on and, as we squint in the brightness of the moment, it takes us a while to begin to see things differently, with fresh eyes – fresh eyes that see Jesus' life, death and resurrection as an ecology of hope for the world.

Crucifixion

The worst thing can only not be the last thing if there is an example of love and life beyond death and judgement. Hope in Jesus is not solely about the actions of good people who have some sort of celebrity status; hope in Jesus is first and foremost the story of the salvation of the world.

It's fair to say that the disciples didn't behave well in the face of Jesus' death. One had conspired to get the action over and done with quickly and, with the blessing of a kiss, betrayed Jesus into the hands of his opponents. Faced with the threat of the Roman army, and knowing that their lives were in danger, most of Jesus' other friends ran. Some stayed in the shadows, but they hid away in fear of being caught and crucified themselves. Their sense of self-preservation outweighed their sense of duty. The closest friend of Jesus, the one Jesus had told would desert him to the soundtrack of a chicken's cluck, fulfilled his painful destiny. As dawn broke, his lies were revealed.

Perhaps they were safer, less of a target for the ruling officials, but the only people to accompany Jesus on his final fast track through court systems and across to the local crucifixion site (itself a rubbish heap outside the city walls) were women. At the end of everything, Jesus was crucified in front of his mum, his best friend and a woman who had splashed oil over his feet at a meal. The people who stuck around with Jesus were the vulnerable, the victim, the disenchanted and the diseased. The people who stuck around with Jesus to the bitter end may not have been the people Jesus wanted to be there; no one wants to be humiliated in front of one's mum. But they were the ones who chose to stay, who perhaps hoped, along with the watching crowd, for one more miracle. They were the ones who had a reason to hope – they knew first-hand. So why not again for Jesus?

But.

Jesus breathed his last.

Hope died.

You can imagine the crowds surrounding this spectacle holding their breath, too; waiting for the worst thing not to be the last thing; expecting some sort of twist – after all, that's what he'd been promising them all along. They had seen it and heard about it before – the dead had been raised, the sick healed, political systems challenged. It had all happened in Jesus' life – so why not now in his death? They waited with bated breath.

The clouds that had filled the sky began to dissipate. The sound of birdsong filled the air once again. A shaft of light made the people blink a little. Nothing had changed. The women began to sob. It wasn't meant to be like this. Everything should have been different. The worst thing was the last thing.

Soon, one by one, the crowds, too, begin to dwindle. There's nothing to see here. No fanfare. No spectacle. No whatever Jesus promised. There were two certainties after all – death and taxes. Both ruling systems had won the day: physiologically and politically.

Even Pilate, having enjoyed his sparring match with the philosopher Jesus, resigned himself to the rest of his evening, feeling a mixture of relief and disappointment that his power had not been superseded in the way everyone had been talking about. But the death of Jesus wasn't blood on his hands. He'd washed his hands of the whole affair, and there were pressing matters of state to get back to.

Jesus was wrong. There was no hope.

The women wept.

The theologian N.T. Wright notes in *Surprised by Hope* (SPCK, 2011):

> The crucifixion of Jesus was the end of all [the disciples'] hopes. Nobody dreamed of saying, 'oh that's all right – he'll be back in a few days.' Nor did anybody say, 'well at least now he's in heaven with God.' They were not looking for that sort of 'kingdom'. After all, Jesus himself had taught them to pray that God's kingdom would come 'on earth as it is in heaven'. What they said… was things like 'we had hoped that he was the one who would redeem Israel' (Luke 24:21), the implication being,

'but they crucified him, so he can't have been'... Crucifixion of a would-be Messiah meant that he wasn't the Messiah, not that he was. When Jesus was crucified, every single disciple knew what it meant: we backed the wrong horse. The game is over. Whatever their expectations, as far as they were concerned hope had crumbled into ashes. They knew they were lucky to escape with their own lives.

Jesus was dead and everything they had hoped for, searched for and given up the family business for was like dust before their very eyes. Their hopeful resistance was over.

It's tempting for us to race to the end of the story – to know that the gospel accounts are full of resurrection hope and promise and thus to fast-forward to encounters with the risen Jesus. But for hope to have credibility and power, there also needs to be absence and despair. Pandora only knew hope at the point at which she felt everything was futile. For there to be any authority in world-changing, another-world-is-possible resurrection hope – there needs to be the opportunity for everything to be meaningless, vapour, fake news.

Pete Greig, director of 24-7 Prayer, writes in *God on Mute* (Kingsway, 2007):

No-one really talks about Holy Saturday, yet if we stop and think about it, it's where most of us live most of our lives. Holy Saturday is the no-man's land between questions and answers, prayers and miracles. It's where we wait – with a peculiar mixture of faith and despair – whenever God is silent, or life doesn't make sense.

The disciples didn't know it then, but the Christian tradition offers us a gift in our own experiences of utter desolation and despair: Holy Saturday, the day when everything comes crashing down and there is only God's absence and hopelessness.

It's easy to jump to the end of the story, to move to the resurrection part of the narrative, confident in Jesus' participation in the muck of life.

A culture of fear, however, is not only about knowing and experiencing the human part of fear, terror and hopelessness. It must also be about living with and working through those times when even God seems to have left the building and left us to it; those times when prayers are not answered, when worship is difficult, when the questions pile up and we can't find a solution; those moments when the news is so devastating it takes our breath away, when we too want to run into the shadows or wash our hands and be done with it all.

The disciples huddled together, sharing their shock and their shame in the sanctuary of seclusion. A culture of fear constantly calls people to withdraw from community and to withhold relationships, yet hope offers a different whisper: an offer of remaining in community and sharing the vulnerability and devastation of the moment. Sit and wait; pause and ponder; tell the ancient stories, as the exiles did; sing the songs of the ancient land; and find a way to move towards a renewed tomorrow. Perhaps there is no hope for tomorrow, but perhaps there is a reason to rely on the present, for there we find the very footprints of God.

The crucifixion of Jesus appeared to rob the whole of the Jesus narrative of its power and hope. The Messiah had been massacred, and God didn't seem to have stepped into the breach. The disciples were left telling the stories of the footsteps they took with Jesus and the hope that they once had – a hope that had given them meaning, a hope that had given them a place in history, a hope eradicated at the end of the cruellest of punishments for an innocent man.

And yet.

The worst thing is never the last thing.

When all else is failing, and when the shame and the pain are overwhelming; when community is the last thing you want to engage with; when there are so many questions it is deafening; when you are numb – then, in the midst of the absence, the questions, the fear and the shame:

Hope resuscitates a dream.
Hope rekindles the imagination.
Hope silences the chaos.
Hope offers life.
Hope is not dead.

On the third day: the length of time Jonah was in the whale; the length of time Jesus was missing from his family as a boy; the length of time Lazarus lay in the tomb. Three days.

And hope begins to put the pieces back together again. The resistance begins.

Resurrection

This time, there is a different end to the story. There is a resurrection hope; a hope that says there is life after death; there is something after the worst thing; life continues and it is different from that which was experienced before.

On the third day, the women went to the tomb to anoint Jesus' body. When they got there, with their spices and herbs and tear-stained faces straining to comprehend this latest cruel twist, they discovered the tomb was empty. The grave was bare. There were folded clothes and an audience of angels. Still they were unsure of what it all meant. It is easy to empathise with their preference to move to the worst-case scenario – that the body had been taken away for some reason. When all hope is lost, it is no surprise that the blame game is played. Something must have happened, and someone must be held responsible. The bile and the anxiety begin to cause adrenalin to course through fragile veins. There are more and more questions.

Until, one by one, they caught a glimpse of the truth. People racked by the memory of the past three days spent their time blaming themselves and others for the situation they found themselves in. Guilty of deceit, desertion, disloyalty and doubt; shamed by their own absence when their friend needed them most; terrified for their own lives – this band of broken brothers and sisters made a life-changing discovery.

The worst thing is never the last thing.

Crucifixion is not a full stop; it's a comma. Death is not the end of the story. Another world is flourishing into existence. It's here and it's future.

> Do not let your hearts be troubled and do not be afraid.
> JOHN 14:27

Jesus. Is. Alive.

Jesus, the divine-human, the one who got his hands and feet dirty, who walked in their shoes, who called them to follow; the person condemned and crucified; the one who promised that this was not the end of the story – Jesus walked again. Time after time, Jesus demonstrated that he was both this-worldly and next-worldly. He broke bread, and he walked through walls. He barbecued fish on the beach, and he walked on water. He navigated difficult passages of scripture, and he disappeared on a cloud. He spoke with tenderness, yet he seemed somewhat unfamiliar, even to those who knew him best.

To the broken-hearted, the terrified and the ashamed, Jesus stepped right back into their world. There is hope – even when the worst thing (un)imaginable has occurred.

Hope does not exist in isolation; it thrives in a community of broken people who are willing to live with the brokenness because it is the source of their healing and future.

Keeping it all together

On a freezing February evening, out on the Icelandic coastline, there was a glimpse of something ethereal in the sky, a silvery shimmer rising high above the clouds. The northern lights were performing their dance, albeit shielded from our view by the snowstorm that set in the next morning. There was something brewing.

So it is with the Christian hope in God's future. There is a sense that God is brewing something new, something utterly familiar and yet completely different to anything we have seen before. There is a present–future tension pulling us in all directions, inviting our participation in the present, and yet also acting as a catalyst, because this world needs prophetic voices of justice to point out that things are not as they should be.

Thus humanity continues to require a hopeful presence: that articulates the sin, shame and fear which are not of God's kingdom; a hopeful presence that notices those glimpses of grace and re-creation, where there is opportunity to turn around or to ponder the majesty of God in the sanctuary of the here and now; and a hopeful presence that also knows this is not the end of the story and that there is a spectacular finale in place. For now we see dimly, but then... well, even the northern lights will pale into insignificance when compared to the hope fulfilled in the new, holy garden city of God.

Questions for discussion

- What is on your bucket list?

- What difference might an ecological rather than an economic metaphor make to your understanding of God's love and justice?

- Which garden do you find the easiest to engage with: Eden, resurrection or the holy garden city? What are some of the implications of this?

- Where can you plant the gospel this week?

- Find a way to experience dark and light this week.

5

Getting our hands and feet dirty

May our Lord Jesus Christ himself and God our Father, who loved us and by his grace gave us eternal encouragement and good hope, encourage your hearts and strengthen you in every good deed and word.

2 THESSALONIANS 2:16–17

For Christians, hope is ultimately hope in Christ. The hope that he really is what for centuries we have been claiming he is. The hope that despite the fact that sin and death still rule the world, he somehow conquered them. The hope that in him and through him all of us stand a chance of somehow conquering them too. The hope that at some unforeseeable time and in some unimaginable way he will return with healing in his wings.

Frederick Buechner, *Wishful Thinking* (Collins, 1972)

Getting our feet wet

It was meant to be a fun family day out, as we and a group of friends headed to an interactive museum. What hadn't been planned for was that, although the day was fine, there had been torrential rain the previous night, so there were puddles everywhere. Thus it came to pass that, almost immediately at the entrance, the toddler met *the* puddle. A determined run-up was followed by an enormous splash.

The toddler, now caked in mud, laughed gleefully as the muddy gloop rose over her wellies and up to her knees. Needless to say, the splashing continued. It was impossible to move her from the entertainment of the puddle. No amount of coaxing, bribery, threat or attempts at physical eviction was successful. We had only got as far as the entrance to the venue! Dripping from head to toe, without a single item of dry clothing remaining, the toddler continued to content herself with the childlike delight of the muck and mud of a single, giant (even to an adult) puddle at the entrance to the open-air museum.

It may not have been the best example of parenting I have exhibited, but I eventually gave up trying to coax the toddler away, and instead opted for the watchful-eye-with-a-mug-of-tea approach. In that moment, the toddler taught me the importance of childlike playfulness. Sometimes joy and a hopeful resistance to fear are found when we dive right in, when we willingly choose to be courageous and get our hands and feet dirty.

Walking in our shoes

In Auschwitz, there is a large room with glass cabinets on either side of a walkway. The room is part of one of the former dormitories. In each cabinet, filled almost two-thirds of the way to the roof, are thousands upon thousands of shoes. They are the shoes of the men, women and children who died during the Holocaust.

At the turn of the last century, the UK received over 1,000 refugees from the war-torn area around Kosovo. Initially received into a central location, arriving with nothing, the families were eventually housed in communities across the country. As a volunteer with that project, I heard time and time again that one of the most difficult things that those most vulnerable people endured was learning to walk in shoes that had belonged to someone else – compassionately donated, indiscriminately passed out and not quite fit for purpose.

From the sanctuary roof in St James' Church, Piccadilly, installation artist Arabella Dorman hung over 700 items of clothing – including shoes – all salvaged from the wreckage of boats eventually run aground on the Greek island of Lesbos. Each item is a symbol of the vain hopes of desperate refugees attempting to enter Europe.

In March 2018, campaigners placed 7,000 pairs of shoes in the grounds of Capitol Hill in the USA, as a silent protest representative of all the children who had lost their lives in gun crimes since the Sandy Hook massacre six years previously.

In May the same year, campaigners for the 'millions missing' campaign placed pairs of shoes in public spaces in 95 cities around the world, calling for greater understanding and action to support those who live with ME. The campaign continues to highlight the challenges faced by those living with the condition, and those who have been discriminated against due to a lack of research, medical investment and understanding of the condition. Each pair of shoes represented someone housebound because of ME.

The incarnation of Jesus has been poetically summarised as 'God walking in our shoes'. It can be easy to reduce this sentiment to images of catwalks and sneakers. However, the idea that Jesus walks in our shoes is far more visceral, transformative and countercultural when stated alongside the experiences noted above. Jesus brought hope into the world because he knew that the world had the potential to be a terrifying place. Jesus 'moved into the neighbourhood' (John 1:14, MSG) to show that there is hope within the human experience, not despite it. Jesus' being 'God with skin on' brings hope that the divine knows our despair, dramas, fears and shame – and has the intent, power, creative imagination and loving care to do something about it.

If Jesus does walk in our shoes, it means that Jesus was walking in the shoes of the Auschwitz resident as they walked down the staircase to the gas showers. It means that Jesus walked in the shoes of the refugees, feet bloodied from their already lengthy journey and then feeling the excruciating pain of seawater on sores. And Jesus was present with those drowned beneath the waves whose shoes washed up on the shore. It means that Jesus was with those children for whom school was not a safe place, and where bullets prematurely cut short their lessons and their lives. It means that Jesus knew the difficulty of walking in shoes that didn't fit.

In this chapter, we will explore Jesus' ministry in terms of his participation in the world, offering hope to those who needed it most. Christian hope is to be found in the person of Jesus: both present gift and future salvation. In turn, hope is to be put into practice, as we too are called to get our hands and feet dirty. We are called to dive into the messier area with delight and playfulness, as well as solidarity.

At first glance, being born in unusual family circumstances, in the stable of a busy hostel, is not the most auspicious entrance for the Saviour of the world to have made. His first crib was a feeding trough, and it's safe to assume that even the best keeper of stable-dwelling animals would not have expected the straw-strewn floor to be clean. Jesus was born to a poor family, tended to in an outside shed and visited by a ragamuffin band of untrustworthy night workers – not to mention a caravan of stargazers who couldn't quite believe that the stars were pointing to this bizarre palace.

Suffice it to say that Jesus was surrounded by a lot of muck, even in his early years. From the sewage in a used stable to the sawdust of Joseph's workshop, Jesus was familiar with mess and muck and mire. Even his death – crucified on the local rubbish heap – acts as a reminder that Jesus modelled a humanity and a humility that was gritty and unafraid of contamination. Through Jesus' hope-bringing participation in the world, God shows that relationship is not meant to be one of clinical sterility – something obtained in isolation away from the dirt and grime of the world – but forged within the difficulties and puddles of life. Jesus offers hope to people who feel tarnished or excluded from society because their lives are messy. Jesus offers hope to those who are contaminated in some way, going out of his way to touch them, talk to them and pull up a pew and eat with them. Jesus offers hope to victims. Ultimately, Jesus offers a hope which declares that however frightening and hopeless the present situation appears, the worst thing is never the last thing. Not even death is the end of the story.

Frederick Buechner, in *The Final Beast* (HarperCollins, 1982), provocatively notes:

> The worst isn't the last thing about the world. It's the next to the last thing. The last thing is the best. It's the power from on high that comes down into the world, that wells up from the rock-bottom worst of the world like a hidden spring. Can you believe it? The last, best thing is the laughing deep in the hearts of the saints, sometimes our hearts even. Yes. You are terribly loved and forgiven.

Jesus' life and death intentionally show that there is hope, even in the worst-case scenario; that the worst thing is never the last thing; that relationship with God and with a wider community of people is not only possible but is also the preferred way of the kingdom of God. In Jesus we find a God-human who desires the whole of humanity to know it is both terribly loved and totally forgiven.

Jesus got his hands and his feet dirty, and time and time again engaged in practices and rituals that unearthed a divine revelation in the midst of the muck. Jesus was not afraid of mess, nor was he reserved in his approach to people who were different from him. This pragmatic and textured aspect to Jesus' life remains undeveloped in 21st-century thinking about the life of Jesus – and yet, as a model of engaged, relational, authentic living, it perhaps gives us the greatest clue about the nature of the kingdom of God, the hope which Jesus brings and the life to which we are thus called.

There are three areas of Jesus' ministry that offer hope to those Jesus encountered, and in which we find a model of world-changing engagement: dirt, debate and dinner.

Dirt

To those who were excluded from relationship and wider society, Jesus' approach was very tactile and visceral. Jesus was not afraid of getting involved with people who were the epitome of messy – those with open sores, women who were bleeding, the dead. Jesus gave hope to those whom society had written off.

Jesus *touched* those who were sick or in need of help. This contravened convention and good order. Jesus was willing to put his own health, welfare and safety below that of those he was engaging with. For example, Jesus touched a number of lepers in a range of circumstances. He was not afraid of the belief that leprosy could be transmitted through touch. Instead, he offered those who were made to feel anxious in community and forced to wear identification of their disease a moment of humanity and a physical connection that they had long forgotten.

Jesus' touch was also a source of healing and wholeness for those needing hope and healing. The woman who had an embarrassing and painful gynaecological problem (Mark 5:25–34; Luke 8:43–48) touched the hem of Jesus' clothing and was healed. Jesus had not instigated conversation with her, and the disciples hadn't even noticed that she had approached them. However, healing occurred, a connection was made and the worst thing was not the last thing. In this story, Jesus was taken by surprise, and a brave woman's life was forever changed.

Hope and healing are not only offered to those who deserve them or who are powerful enough to feel entitled to them. Even with the most excluded and marginalised people, on numerous occasions

Jesus refused to conform to expectations, and healing came through physical encounter and touch. This includes those who were demon possessed and friends who were sick or dying (or, in the case of Lazarus, already dead), and it is crucial in the case of a paralysed man who is not only touched by Jesus but is manhandled on to a rooftop before being told to pick up his mat and walk for the first time in decades.

On three separate occasions – with a deaf and mute man, an unnamed blind man and a blind man named Bartimaeus – Jesus used a combination of touch and spit, and for Bartimaeus even mud, to bring about their restoration. There is evidence to suggest that this mirrored a practice from some of the other magic workers and faith-healers of the day, so this was perhaps not as strange as it seems to a contemporary reader. This demonstrates not only that Jesus told stories which incorporated local knowledge but also that he used the practices employed by others in order to bring healing, hope and transformation out of the mire of despair and hopelessness.

Hopeful resistance makes the mundane holy. By being tactile, as well as incorporating quasi-medical techniques from the ancient world, Jesus offered hope to those who had been let down in the past by medical professionals and by wider society. He treated people with dignity and respect and took the opportunity to build a connection and a relationship with those whom the rest of society were seeking to exclude. Jesus was not afraid of getting 'dirty' – be that literal or metaphorical.

In 1987, Diana Princess of Wales caused an international outcry when she touched and kissed a young boy diagnosed with HIV without any form of barrier or protection. It was an image that defined her and has changed the way HIV care has developed over the subsequent decades.

Touch offers hope to those who are at the powerless mercy of stigma and misunderstanding, especially those with illnesses that can be difficult to both diagnose and treat. Pastoral touch, and Jesus' more primitive methods of saliva and soil, offer a countercultural vision of God's care and compassion, as well as modelling a pattern of behaviour that is respectful of the dignity and humanity of others. Even before oxytocin was identified as the 'feel-good' hormone, and scientists discovered the physical and psychological benefits of touch, Jesus broke with all social conventions and sought to build people up in the fullness of their humanity.

Debate

Jesus was not afraid to argue with the powerful in defence of those who were contaminated or considered sinful or who were shamed in some, often very public, way. Jesus offers hope to those whom society sought to shame, by honouring them and standing up for them.

When a woman was at risk of being stoned to death because she had been caught in a honeytrap, Jesus didn't participate in the public shaming of the woman. Surrounded by a crowd standing in judgement against her, Jesus bent down and doodled in the dust. Instead of giving those in authority the permission to further abuse the woman's body, Jesus paused and wrote in the sand. Hope was offered to a guilty woman because, as Jesus pointed out, everyone is sinful and could be publicly shamed in the same way as her – but who wants to be in the position of being caught out and becoming the next piece of target practice for the stone-throwers?

Hope never throws the first stone, but stays until the end of the action. The worst thing is never the last thing.

A gatecrasher at a party Jesus was attending took a precious vase of perfume. Its value has been estimated to equate to her dowry. To the chagrin of the watching crowd of invited guests, the woman – often caricatured as being of ill-repute – opened the jar and poured the ointment over Jesus. The onlookers were uncomfortable and awkward. One friend broke the silence and loudly whispered his distaste at what was happening. If she was to be so profligate with her possessions, then surely the vial could have achieved greater impact if it had been invested or sold, rather than used to anoint Jesus. After all, not even Jesus was worth that much, surely.

Jesus instead showed that hope accepts gifts that are offered. Jesus' willingness to get dirty and to join the debate enabled one disciple to do something about the dirt in return. The aroma of perfume filled a room otherwise soured with sweat and grime. Hope isn't afraid of debate and disagreement – but, like the lingering scent of expensive perfume, it changes the atmosphere of a room. Hope is intimate and vulnerable. The woman could have been humiliated in her act. Instead, Jesus raised her up, acknowledged and received her gift, and blessed her activity. Through a broken vessel, the aroma of hope filled the room – much like Pandora, if you think about it.

Whether she was a serial wife or merely unfortunate, a midday encounter with Jesus at the local watering hole enabled one shamed and disgraced community member to become the first evangelist in town. In the heat of the day, when no one would want to be fetching pails of water, Jesus once again broke all cultural convention: a man meeting with a woman at a deserted location; a single man meeting a several times married woman; a respectable man meeting with a woman whose current personal circumstances meant that she was the source of gossip in the village, a fact underlined by her midday excursion so as to avoid the whispers; a Jew meeting with a Gentile. This encounter should not have happened. Jesus should have done the honourable thing and walked away. If Jesus didn't, then he should at the very least have behaved in a more entitled way. After all, he had the social and cultural upper hand, which is exactly why the woman reacted when Jesus asked her to pour him a drink. Entitled. Patriarchal. A product of the system that said that a man was to be obeyed, no matter the cost – a cost she had likely paid time and time again in her previous relationships. Yet their verbal sparring quickly turned from bitterness and spite to hope and grace for a woman so often shunned and shamed. Jesus did not leave her as a victim, signed up to an early version of the #metoo campaign. Instead, he offered her the source of life. Hope. He put her right back on track and into the heart of community. Whereas once the woman was pushed aside by her neighbours, this strange encounter at the local well resourced her to rebuild fractured relationships and to regain her identity within her context. People began to take her seriously again. This unnamed woman discovered liberation through living water.

Hope in her midst saw an outcast thrust back into the heart of her community – from the well to the marketplace. Hope did not see a victim of circumstance. Hope took the time to hear a story and offered an alternative ending. There was sparring and a debate – but the result of the discourse was restored relationships, rebuilt confidence and the bubbling spring of the kingdom of God at work.

Throughout scripture, Jesus noticed those who were made to be victims of their own circumstances and, often in controversial and countercultural ways, sided with them against the prosecutors of the day. Jesus publicly debated those in authority and conversed with those who were normally excluded. Jesus offered hope, grace, dignity, humanity and healing to those whom the rest of wider society wanted to exclude, excommunicate and extinguish.

Such actions in Jesus' life are also the vehicle through which Jesus' death and resurrection would provide the ultimate hope for the world. Hope is not afraid of shame or fear or brokenness – but hope also offers a way forward so that victims become survivors. Hopeful resistance challenges the rules and enables those on the margins to be seen, heard, loved.

Jesus turned a debate into the opportunity for people to be heard and for their story to be told in all its vulnerability. It's perhaps no surprise that the connection between storytelling and life-giving vulnerability is becoming more and more popular in the social sciences and therapeutic communities. Professor Brené Brown in her groundbreaking work in this area describes her discovery:

> In the process of collecting thousands of stories from diverse men and women... ranging from eighteen to eighty-seven – I saw new patterns that I wanted to know more about. We all struggle with shame and the fear of not being enough... Many of us are afraid to let our true selves be seen and known. But in this huge mound of data there was also story after story of people living these amazing and inspirational lives... Wholeheartedness is as much about embracing our tenderness and vulnerability as it is about developing knowledge and claiming power.

Brown's conclusion is stark: in order to move from being a victim defined by a story and experience of shame, one needs to embrace vulnerability and to live more compassionately, creatively, connectedly and courageously – more hopefully. Jesus modelled this before it became vogue. Jesus engaged with people in despair and fear, and he enabled them to become powerful survivors, storytellers, disciples and community leaders in their own right, *because* of the hope in their story, not despite it.

Dinner

Hope which is silent is not hope at all. Hope does not sit on the sidelines, waiting for systems to change. Hope is not passive, and the hope that Jesus offered to anyone who would listen was certainly not ignorant of the need for action. In a culture of fear, the temptation is to become anaesthetised to the needs that appear to be everywhere and to become ambivalent to people and situations. Hope dances in puddles and stands up to bullies. Hope pulls up a chair, breaks bread and invites people to feast. Jesus' ministry brought hope through healing, through dialogue and through feasts.

Jesus had a habit of eating with people who were despised and rejected by the locals. Such behaviour did not go unnoticed and did not go down well. Zacchaeus was in the pocket of the Roman officials. A chief tax collector, he was excellent at his job, fiddling the books so that he was able to make the most amount of profit from those under his direction. Why would Jesus want to spend time with someone who had dodgy business ethics and whom everyone else jostled out of the picture?

Resourcefully, Zacchaeus, small in stature and struggling to catch a glimpse of the celebrity Jesus in town, saw his opportunity and climbed a tree as Jesus rode through the town. Jesus was unafraid of political systems, politicians and even the dubious practices of tax collectors in trees. Jesus called Zacchaeus out and, rather forwardly, invited himself to dinner. Once again, Jesus' engagement came with a visceral action – let's eat together and see what happens; let's be equals around a dining table and begin to sketch what a different world view might look like. To the distaste and disappointment of the disbelieving onlooking crowd, Zacchaeus ran home to prepare a meal. Jesus sullied himself in the company of a rogue, and the onlookers were understandably disapproving. The tax collector was tantamount to a thief, yet Jesus decided that he was the person he wanted to meet and the tax system was the thing that he wanted to challenge. Outrageous!

The result of this encounter, however, was that Zacchaeus' transformation began. A new tax code was written. Where people had been defrauded, Zacchaeus paid them back. Where there was injustice, mercy sprang forth. Hope says that not even the political systems of the day are beyond the grasp of grace. Even short people with a penchant for petty larceny are challenged and changed in conversation with Jesus, and in turn, the people were reimbursed for their losses over the years Zacchaeus had been in charge.

Hope is found in broken bread and over a dinner table.

Ultimately, Jesus offers a hope which declares that however frightening and hopeless the present situation appears, the worst thing is
never the last thing. Death is not the end of the story.

Two distraught sisters, having trusted that Jesus could change the
world, suddenly realised that perhaps Jesus wasn't who they thought
he was. Jesus showed up too late to save their brother, so instead of
helping his friends, Jesus was faced with their righteous anger. They
felt entitled to some of the miraculous interventions that Jesus had
shown other people – strangers. Why didn't he show up for his friends
like he did for everyone else?

The sisters were angry, upset and full of grief. This sentiment was
shared by Jesus, who in a moment of profound emotion, approached
the cold, lifeless body of his friend, and wept. The villagers were
out in force, offering their own rituals of bereavement. This was
not a silent scene, and Jesus' tears were submerged beneath the
outpouring of grief around him.

Yet there was something else stirring. The worst thing – death in
this case – cannot have the final say. Hope needs to make a home
in the place of despair. So Jesus did what he could. He asked for the
stone to be rolled away. He risked the stench of death and instead
trusted that there was the possibility of a different ending. This was a
divinely appointed resuscitation of a recently passed cadaver. Jesus
spoke. 'Lazarus come out' echoed around the stone cave where the
body had been laid. With that, Lazarus lived, his exit from the tomb
still shrouded in the mystery of his grave clothes.

Jesus had received criticism and anger, showed compassion and still
offered hope amid the very worst thing. Jesus offered to his closest
friends the opportunity to see and trust that whatever was to come
in the future, the worst things to come would not be the last things.

Another world is possible. Just wait and see.

> Praise be to the God and Father of our Lord Jesus Christ! In his great mercy he has given us new birth into a living hope through the resurrection of Jesus Christ from the dead, and into an inheritance that can never perish, spoil or fade.
>
> 1 PETER 1:3–4

In the dirt, hope brings healing. In debate, hope restores identity and relationship. At dinner, hope makes things right. In death, hope says it's not the end.

Jesus' ministry was tactile and visceral, messy and countercultural. Through Jesus' model of ministry with the marginalised, poor, disadvantaged and rejected, disciples today are shown how to live as ambassadors of living hope, striving to change the world. Jesus got his hands and his feet dirty. He walked in our shoes and challenged human systems. He called out truth to power and didn't resist opportunities for dialogue, even when his perspectives were so wholly distasteful to his audience.

Fear shies away from engagement. Fear gives way. Fear resists change. Fear doesn't want a different opinion. Fear always makes the world smaller.

Hope, however. Hope eats meals with fraudsters. Hope tells more stories and invites more and more people around the table. Hope challenges the belief that nothing can be done. Hope never lets the worst thing be the last thing, for other people as well as for ourselves. Hope shown in the ministry of Jesus is the model of our discipleship.

Watering the flowers

At 1.00 am on 14 June 2017, a fire ripped through a social housing tower block in the centre of London, killing 72 people and leaving hundreds with life-limiting injuries and ongoing debilitating mental health issues. The devastation caused by the fire, images of which have become iconic, was the result of decades of catastrophic systematic failure.

Amid the consequent social unrest, political infighting, blame, inquiries, medical appointments and ongoing anger and frustration of residents, hope began to be seen in unexpected places: from the vanloads of goods and gifts being donated to the survivors to the local *Big Issue* seller laying a bunch of flowers (picked from nearby gardens) on a makeshift memorial.

Sometimes, in order to offer hope where there are only questions, there needs to be a simple, prophetic action that cuts through the politics and begins to reach the hearts of those in need – whoever they are. Cathy and Miranda did just this. Two days after the fire was extinguished, the physical ash settling but the embers of emotion beginning to flare, Cathy and Miranda began to water the flowers that had been left in memoriam. Together they spent hours tending to the flowers – and listening to the people who came up to them, just needing to be heard. As the *New Statesman* reported:

> 'This is not just a nice display,' Cathy says while watering the flowers. 'A lot of people come because they need somebody to talk to, they might need some counselling or they might need some help. Lots of them don't want to walk into a church but they will always speak to a woman who is tending flowers.'

Cathy (a local clergy spouse) and Miranda got their hands and feet dirty in a community covered in the ashes of tragedy. They got involved: watering the flowers that had been tied to the railings of the devastated building and its surroundings. They were present to the pain of the community, and they listened to the stories of the people when the powerbrokers did not. For a few vital days, hope – Jesus – looked like two women watering the flowers.

Jesus constantly drew crowds, engaged in conversation and challenged authority. He used what was around him to craft stories or to forge the means of healing. Hope offered through this relational, transformational, system-shaking, world-view-changing example didn't come with a manual or strategy document. Instead, hope whispered in the background, worked in the shadows, brought two women and a watering can to a disaster zone. The hope Jesus offered to his disciples and to us becomes the invitation to get our hands and feet dirty and our prejudices challenged. As the kingdom of God continues to expand, more and more storytellers, story-keepers and flower arrangers (to name but a few) are invited around the table and into the divine dance of Christian hope.

Sometimes hope looks like watering the flowers.

Getting your hands and feet dirty

The theologian Jürgen Moltmann, in *Theology of Hope* (SCM, 2010), explores the difference that this post-crucifixion, living-in-resurrection-technicolour hope offers:

> Christian hope is resurrection hope, and it proves its truth in the contradiction of the future prospects thereby offered and guaranteed for righteousness as opposed to death, glory as opposed to suffering, peace as opposed to dissension.

In other words, to the disciples, Jesus says, 'You ain't seen nothing yet.' To the Jesus-follower of today, the promise is the same – this is only part of the story. The worst thing isn't the last thing. Take a walk in my footprints and let's see what hope tomorrow brings with it.

Living in the mess and the dirt can lead to protest and justice. A model of debate and dialogue can lead to solidarity. An open dinner table can inspire creativity and beauty.

Dirt: protest and justice

For far too long, the western Christian church has remained tangled in the tension between conversion evangelism and social-justice action. This dichotomy has been perpetuated over the last century by, on the one hand, well-meaning evangelistic rallies offering a personal salvation plan and, on the other, the rise of liberation theology and a social gospel.

An 'on earth as it is in heaven' agenda necessarily sees proclamation and justice as being in partnership with one another. Indeed, they should never have been so acrimoniously divorced in the first place. The hopeful promise of the kingdom of God is a revolutionary one. It's the very reason Jesus was crucified in the first place – the transformation he offered to a fragile and broken world challenged the power brokers and principalities of his day, as well as the spiritual forces he constantly overthrew. Jesus demonstrated time and time again that God was turning the world upside down and that change was coming from within, not without.

Hope, therefore, finds its place in protest movements, in social-justice campaigns and in the midst of revolutions. Systemic and ethical issues within contemporary society become the vehicle of transformation and an opportunity to live in the kingdom of God, in the here and now – and for that to be a tangible reality for others too. Anti-debt campaigns; climate change and environmental stewardship initiatives; anti-discrimination and anti-abuse campaigns; programmes to care for the homeless and provide food banks – these are not the added extras of church life. Instead, they are the lifeblood of the kingdom.

Justice brings with it conflict and debate. It incites people's passions on all sides, and it requires determination, courage and compassion to mould anger into productive and tangible results. Justice is a gut-wrenching, blood-sweat-and-tears-inducing, sleepless-night-causing, flag-waving scream from the barricades. Protest speaks up for the poor and the excluded. It offers love where there is often hate. It caresses despair and enables those vilified to experience dignity. Protest and justice speak up and show up when immigrant children are separated from their parents, or when refugees are turned out of their makeshift shelters in case they are getting too comfortable. Protest and justice say that it shouldn't be like this and that there is a hopeful vision of a future where it isn't.

Hope-filled actions can be small-scale rebellions against the status quo or enormous campaigns for the global good, but they are actions all the same. Living in resurrection hope is about living in the tension that the world is not right but that humanity has the ability to partner with the Spirit in bringing about a revolution of hope.

The heart of the gospel is grounded in the example of Jesus to challenge those in power, to act on behalf of those who are weaker or different, and the call to get involved in a resurrection movement of hope and kingdom-change in the present day.

Hope does not deny the complexity of social, moral and ethical issues. The gospel is always expansive, always open to the influence of the other in order to build relationships and understanding. Another world is possible. It doesn't have to be like this. The worst thing is never the last thing. Resurrection hope looks different from what we know now. Hope provides the courage to stand up, to walk in the shoes of another and to find ways of living and loving in the expanse of the good news of Jesus.

Debate: solidarity and love

Hope in the present circumstances reaches beyond the inevitability of despair and towards a deeper sense of solidarity, both with other humans and with the heavens. Whereas justice has that sense of high-octane, world-changing protest and revolution, solidarity acts as a collaborative counterbalance.

Solidarity sits alongside those in need and listens to their story.

Solidarity speaks wisdom into the silence of hopeless despair, bringing comfort and offering transformation.

Solidarity acts out of personal contemplation and experience, recognising that our own scars of despair and agony can be the source of healing for those wounded in the world's wake.

Solidarity offers the 'balm of Gilead' into the woundedness of the world, declaring that resurrection hope is offered with the open-handed stigmata of crucifixion still raw to the touch.

Solidarity is about our own spiritual lives. Solidarity is also entirely preoccupied with the lived experience of others. It is a flow between the inward and the outward life that is also both entirely present and yet focused on the on-earth-as-in-heaven dimension of the kingdom of God in our daily experience.

Again, this present-here-and-now kingdom-on-earth experience of solidarity is not passive. It is highly engaged, often exhausting and a richly spiritual exercise. Solidarity comes out of a spirituality of presence, practised both as a personal endeavour and as a community of the faithful.

In *Letters from the Desert* (DLT, 1972), the hermit and mystic Carlo Caretto writes:

> Love [we may want to add resurrection hope] is the synthesis of contemplation and action, the meeting-point between heaven and earth, between God and humanity.

Caretto, recognising that there is a paradox between this over-whelming sense of participating in justice and spiritual reflexivity, speaks of the need to perceive those 'thin place' moments of heaven touching earth in the here and now. Loving, hopeful action leads to contemplation, and from contemplation, action and engagement find their energy reserve. There is a flow and a movement between the inner and outer life that is required if one is both to live hopefully and to seek hope in the midst of lived experience. In order to be proactive for the kingdom in the present age, one needs to be a contemplative as well as deeply engaged in the world.

Solidarity, therefore, offers hope in the mix and midst of fear and despair, by enabling an individual to be their best selves, and providing the space and context into which others' despair can be hosted, heard and healed. As Brian Draper writes in *Soulfulness* (Hodder and Stoughton, 2016):

> We can discover more of our own uniqueness and express this lovingly and purposefully through our actions. I don't want to be stuck in a soulless rut. I want to find the soulful groove, learn to live with energy and creativity, and in the process become a positive, engaging part of the solution at a troubled time.

This soulful, hopeful, centred, groovy way of being provides the energy and inspiration for meaningful action. Living and loving in Christian hope is about becoming part of the 'solution at a troubled time' in such a way that action and activity engage with the heaven-on-earth dimension of life today. Hopeful resistance is about living soulfully, authentically and truthfully.

Some of the most soulful people are also the most wounded people, but they have learnt in some way to continue to live fully, presently and hopefully amid their pain and their despair. Even in these circumstances, a resurrection hope does not look fleetingly towards a future time when pain will be eradicated. Instead, resurrection hope embraces the experiences, names them and talks about them. Emotions flow, and still there is a deeper hope beneath the surface. This hope is not defeated by the personal, communal or global tragedy and despair – but is found in living with the knowledge that in Jesus, the kingdom is here.

Hopeful solidarity is about leaning *into* the pain and suffering of another, be it a neighbour or a stranger. Hope is eternally patient, and to offer that sacred space for a heaven-meeting-earth revelation is the most vital of eschatological callings for individuals and the church.

Eugene Peterson, in *Five Smooth Stones for Pastoral Work* (Eerdmans, 1996), writes:

> [Our] work joins the sufferer, shares the experience of God's anger, enters into the pain, the hurt, the sense of absurdity, the descent into the depths. It is not [our] task… to alleviate suffering, to minimise it or to mitigate it, but to share it after the example of our Lord Messiah… By doing that, a person [is assisted] to intensify a capacity for suffering, enables a person to 'lean into the pain.' Writing cheerful graffiti on the rocks in the valley of deep shadows is no substitute for companionship with the person who must walk in the darkness.

Solidarity and spirituality are therefore about discovering hope alongside others, and living faithfully during our own despair as well as the world's hopelessness.

By deeply engaging with the situation of another and enabling both parties to 'lean in', the kingdom of God can begin to do its recalibration and redemptive work. Hopeful solidarity releases us from the expectation that we must have all the answers, that in some way we are the ones who need to fix every situation. 'On earth as it is in heaven' means that any outcome, transition, transformation or change is as a result of God's involvement and not our own.

For the 21st century, this is hugely liberating and captivating. Solidarity is about showing up. What happens next is up to God.

Dinner: the art of creativity

Amid a meaningless, despair-ridden, pain-filled, hopeless existence, being creative and engaging with the arts can appear to be the most frivolous, self-indulgent, bourgeois response. There has been a significant inheritance of the concept of 'high' or fine art, which only an elite few can access. However, creativity is at the heart of the gospel. Creativity sees the status quo and then finds a way to subvert it – for this current experience is not the end of the story. Another world is possible, and humanity has the tools and resources to begin to shape something different, something of life, in the here and now.

Hope and a vision of a renewed future are offered in the words of poets and in the graffiti of protest, in the final brush-flourishes of a canvas and in the rhythm of a crafted piece of music – even in the subway in Washington. Creativity, born ultimately out of the central feature of God's own character (after all, in the beginning was God, and God… created!), offers the means of resuscitation to a dying world. Noticing beauty expands our thinking and our awareness of the present state of being. Creativity is a release valve for the kingdom of God, exploding a new way of being, often changing the atmosphere of a situation, which in turn enables something of the hope within the kingdom of God to crack into the environment.

Hope can be offered in a craftivist project, sending knitted angels to Parliament to ask for a change in the benefits system.

Hope can be offered in painted stones, hidden around a market town as a way of blessing those who find them and pick them up.

Hope can be offered in the entrepreneur of the shoe company that sells designer items to provide clothing for the disadvantaged.

Hope can be offered in the circle of cushions on the floor of a yurt, as a listening place is opened up to help a fractured community find a way forwards.

Hope can be offered in the community garden, built on a derelict sewage works.

Hope can be offered in the café that uses discarded or locally grown products in order to serve a meal to anyone who is hungry.

Hope can be shared in a referral to a food bank, as dinner is served to a hungry family.

Hope can be offered in the women watering the flowers, left in memoriam at the site of a devastating fire.

Hope can be offered, meaning that the love of God in Christ – the divine flow of all things – can be found.

Hopeful resistance is everywhere. There is a choice to be made. Is the world today meant to be experienced as a cold, tortured place of meaninglessness and despair? Or is there, in the words of Paul writing to the Romans, a groaning at the heart of creation that is desperate to offer an alternative?

> For the creation was subjected to frustration, not by its own choice, but by the will of the one who subjected it, in hope that the creation itself will be liberated from its bondage to decay and brought into the freedom and glory of the children of God. We know that the whole creation has been groaning as in the pains of childbirth right up to the present time. Not only so, but we ourselves, who have the firstfruits of the Spirit, groan inwardly as we wait eagerly for our adoption to sonship, the redemption of our bodies. For in this hope we were saved. But hope that is seen is no hope at all. Who hopes for what they already have? But if we hope for what we do not yet have, we wait for it patiently.
> ROMANS 8:20–25

Creativity is, therefore, part of the invitation to participate in, and co-create with the Spirit, the kingdom of God in the present age. Creativity and recreation are key to living hopefully in an age of fear.

Cultural anthropologist Brené Brown talks of creativity as 'meaning making'. This can be a very liberating view of Christian hope: a way of helping humanity make meaning in the midst of meaninglessness. Brown's view is that creativity is such a significant part of being human that it is the one thing which can help to make sense of any given situation. As she writes in *The Gifts of Imperfection* (Hazelden, 2010):

> Let me sum up what I've learned about creativity:
>
> 1 'I'm not very creative' doesn't work. There's no such thing as creative people and non-creative people. There are only people who use their creativity, and people who don't. Unused creativity doesn't just disappear. It lives within us until it's expressed, neglected to death, or suffocated by resentment and fear.
>
> 2 The only unique contribution that we will ever make in this world will be born out of creativity.
>
> 3 If we want to make meaning, we need to make art. Cook, write, draw, doodle, paint, scrapbook, take pictures, collage, knit, rebuild an engine, sculpt, dance, decorate, act, sing – it doesn't matter. As long as we're creating, we're cultivating meaning.

By experiencing the present-day, 'on earth as it is in heaven' nature of the kingdom of God, hope expressed in creativity enables us to see beyond ourselves and point to a different reality; to make meaning. Hope is a creative resistance movement against despair and fear, calling humanity into a future not yet imaginable. Just as Jesus' incarnation meant that he got his hands and feet dirty – so too are we called to embody a faith that is mucky and messy.

Once we have discovered hope in Jesus for ourselves, once we have discovered the love that flows as the source of all things and that calls us forth into the kingdom of God, we are also called to proactive discipleship. Our calling is to be hope-filled and hope-full people who pay attention, who notice the kingdom of God in our midst and who embody practices that change the world. Jesus' model of ministry – a hopeful resistance of dirt, debate, dinner and the promise to live life to the full this side of eternity – offers us a model for our own Christian engagement and hope-filled resistance to a culture of fear. We find hope in Jesus' model of ministry: doing justice, loving in solidarity and living creatively.

Questions for discussion

- How does it feel to walk in someone else's shoes? How does this shape your understanding of Jesus' walking in our shoes?

- How do you feel about Jesus' tactile and visceral engagement with people? How does this inform your own ministerial practices? What might get in the way?

- Which is most important for you – Jesus' life, death or resurrection? Why?

- Where do you need to get your hands and feet dirtier in your local community?

- Who could you invite for dinner? Do it!

6

Turning the world upside down

May the God of hope fill you with all joy and peace as you trust in him, so that you may overflow with hope by the power of the Holy Spirit.

ROMANS 15:13

It seems to everyone who enjoys the sun's warmth that he is the only one receiving it, but the sun's radiance lights up the whole earth and sea and dissolves together with the sky. In the same way the Spirit seems unique to everyone in whom He abides, but all His grace pours down on everyone. Everyone enjoys this grace to the greatest degree he is capable of, and not to the greatest degree which is possible for the Spirit.

Basil the Great

Sometimes you have to stop and listen to the music

On 12 January 2007, in a mall just outside L'Enfant Plaza metro station in Washington DC, *The Washington Post* ran an experiment for 45 minutes. The experiment parameters were simple – in a banal, seemingly ordinary space, at rush hour, would it be possible to enable commuters and passers-by to notice beauty in their midst?

Dressed in ordinary clothes, a lone performer pulled out a violin and began to play to the wandering masses. In the course of the 45 minutes, 1,097 people passed by the performer. In a collection box at his feet, a total of $32.17 was thrown towards him. Of the 1,097 people, 37 people stopped to listen, although no one stayed for the whole performance.

So far, it's a story that is repeated in public squares and train platforms the world over. However, *The Washington Post* had a twist to this story. Beauty, after all, can interrupt anyone's life or commute, but the challenge is whether we are able to notice it and respond to it. The twist was that the violin being played was a Stradivarius, reputedly worth over $3.5 million. The performer – paid $32.17 for his six pieces of music that January morning – had only days previously performed at a sell-out concert, with tickets retailing at over $100 each. He was one of the greatest violinists of the century: Joshua Bell. Thirty-seven people chose to notice beauty that morning. Only one person recognised Bell.

Sometimes you have to stop and listen to the music.

Sometimes hope, mystery and beauty are found within the ordinary.

Sometimes the most exquisite gifts are to be discovered on street corners and in gutters, rather than in ornate venues with ticket sales.

The Washington Post wanted to experiment and see if people were able to notice and respond to beauty at a time and place when they were preoccupied with going elsewhere. Bell's music danced on the biting breeze of that January morning, bringing beauty into the banal. If only people would stop, pay attention and notice the performance of beauty all around. Annie Dillard, in *Pilgrim at Tinker Creek* (Canterbury, 2011), makes a similar observation, in characteristically eloquent fashion, about the work of the Holy Spirit:

> The answer must be, I think, that beauty and grace [the things
> of the Spirit] are performed whether or not we will sense them.
> The least we can do is try to be there.

The Holy Spirit is the divine flow of all things, the divine presence in otherwise busy days. We are called to pay attention to what is already present. To participate in the divine flow, and to live in line with the Holy Spirit, is to live a life of love. No more, no less.

Occasionally it takes the provocation of a social experiment, and the courage of another performer, to help humanity recognise that there is more to life than the rush of a commute. At other times, as Dillard suggests, such moments are missed, despite them being present all around us. This chapter seeks to expose us afresh to the outrageous beauty of the kingdom of God, as the Holy Spirit dances within the fabric of the universe. Hopeful resistance is paying attention as the world is turned upside down.

Sometimes in our banal, fear-ridden, hopeless world, we have to stop and listen to the music and notice that hope is drifting on the breeze, offering Spirit-guided, hopeful resistance to the lifeless and limiting world we so often choose to inhabit. Sometimes we need help in discovering again what this looks like. Like retuning an old radio so that it receives a clear signal (and I'm just old enough to remember doing the same for black-and-white televisions with portable aerials), the challenge faced by the whole of humanity is to find ways to be tuned in to the things of beauty – the divine flow within everything.

Testimonies of personal, transformative experiences through the work of the Holy Spirit remain the lifeblood of the Christian movement. Stories of broken people discovering their true calling or their identity as a chosen and called child of God continue to be the backbone of Christian community. The creative arts, themselves vehicles for the Holy Spirit's performance, continue to be a catalyst for conversation and change – at the personal as well as societal level. Hope, beauty, love and grace are discovered as people pay attention and play their part in their performance. People are discovering ancient ways of spiritual reflection and discipline that are enabling a reimagination of the spiritual life today. There is renewed interest in retreats, simplicity in worship, small group studies rather than concert-style performance, and rhythms or patterns to daily life that take note of the present and engage with the pattern of creation. Hopeful resistance through the work and inspiration of the Holy Spirit brings forth justice and, in so doing, changes the world.

Faith is not merely an argument to be won and a theory to be understood. Instead, the Holy Spirit requires faith to be something experienced and lived out in practice. This is what hope inspires: provocative, proactive, prophetic people, stepping out of their comfort zones into participation in the kingdom of God. The Holy Spirit is not confined by church walls, nor limited by the vision of church employees. The Holy Spirit is the divine flow within the whole of creation, the love that binds all things together and through which all things have their source. It is this love, the source of all, that seals Christian hope in a culture of fear.

A biblical view of the Holy Spirit

In a world of increasing fear and tension, the Spirit demonstrates the ways in which God remains engaged and ever-present in the world. The Spirit constantly brings relationships together, constantly leads people into a deeper relationship with the divine and constantly calls, equips and enables people to be the best version of themselves. Richard Rohr has described the Holy Spirit as 'implanted hope'. This implanted hope purifies that which is defiled, brings life where there is breathlessness, heals, protects, is a bearer of peace, is powerful and intimate, discovers truth and stands up for the other. The Holy Spirit is the ultimate hope-bringer and life-giver.

The Bible uses a range of metaphors to describe the Spirit's work in the world throughout history. Although imperfect, these metaphors help to shape the understanding of the nature of the Spirit and the Spirit's impact on our lives and the world around us. Metaphors help explore concepts that are hard to grasp, or they seek to speak of what is otherwise indescribable. So it is with the Holy Spirit. The Bible resorts to symbol and metaphor in order to describe the undefinable.

Fire

The Spirit was present in the burning bush, claiming Moses' attention at the beginning of his commission to speak liberation to God's people and to lead them into the promised land. Furthermore, the Spirit then became a torch by which the Hebrew people could see the way for them during the long nights of their exodus. At Pentecost, in a direct parallel with these Exodus accounts, the Holy Spirit is described as descending like tongues of fire over the people. As fire, the Spirit is both uncontainable and makes things pure in the burning.

Breath

The Hebrew word *ruach* is most often translated as 'breath' or 'Spirit'. It is used over 400 times in the Hebrew scriptures. At its most basic, *ruach* means a 'disturbance of the air' (Phyllis Tickle, *The Age of the Spirit*, Baker, 2014), which again recognises the independence of the Spirit from any ulterior control. It is also deeply intimate, dwelling deep within all life.

Water

This metaphor is popular in John's gospel, as the Spirit is associated with   water for the Samaritan woman at the well under the midday sun, as well as for the inquisitive religious leader Nicodemus under the midnight moonlight. The water of the Spirit brings healing and a deepened sense of unity into fractured relationships, including between different ethnic groups (the Samaritans hated the Jews and vice versa). The living water of the Spirit also parallels the rivers flowing through the gardens in Eden and at the end of time (of which more will be explored in the next chapter).

Cloud

Moses encountered the Holy Spirit as a cloud on a number of occasions. When God revealed their identity to Moses on the mountain, the mountain was covered in a cloud and the revelation was accompanied by thunder. When the law was given to the people, Mount Sinai was surrounded by the cloud of the Holy Spirit. When the people were walking through the wilderness, led by fire at night, the Spirit was revealed as a cloud of smoke during the day. This was further mirrored on the mountain of the transfiguration, as Jesus talked with Elijah and Moses. The Spirit offered close protection to those who had permission to spend time in God's presence. This was also the case when the Spirit descended over the temple like a cloud at its dedication (1 Kings 8), and the Spirit was also present within the inner courts of the temple in the time of the prophet Ezekiel (Ezekiel 10:3–4).

Dove

At his baptism, Jesus was taken to the River Jordan, whereupon the Holy Spirit descended upon him like a dove. Parallels can be made with the promise of peace and reconciliation between God and humanity offered to Noah following the catastrophe of the flood, and also with the hovering of the Spirit over the waters prior to creation. The Holy Spirit as a dove brings the message of peace.

Wind

To Elijah, God's voice was not to be found in the storm, but in the silence and space of a whisper in the wind. As such, it commands close attention. At Pentecost, the Spirit was described as sounding like a fierce wind, rushing through the upper room. Closely connected to the metaphor of breath, the symbol of wind speaks of ferocity and gentleness in paradoxical tension.

Legal counsel

In John's gospel, Jesus promised his friends that they would receive the Spirit, the counsel or advocate, when he left them. This is the language of the courtroom, with the advocate or counsel offering a defence on behalf of their client. The Holy Spirit, therefore, stands alongside humanity and speaks up for us, supporting us and acting on our behalf. The Spirit speaks the truth, but also expects and equips humanity to be the very best that we can be.

Oil

In the time of the monarchy, the Hebrew people used oil to anoint their rulers. Oil became a holy symbol of the Spirit, still used in coronation ceremonies today. The Spirit, represented by oil, was also at the heart of the ritual of anointing the sick – a symbolic action as instructed in James 5:14–15. Oil is a symbol of the Spirit's anointing, for leadership and for healing.

Each of these symbolic images demonstrates the Spirit's movement and participation and performance in the world. They provide an imperfect, yet helpful, description of the Spirit's activity. Uncontainable. Uncontrollable. Powerful. Wild. Organic. Mysterious.

The Bible contains account after account of implanted hope in the hearts of broken people, broken society and broken cultures, and it is to two of these encounters that we now turn.

Joel, Acts and the Holy Spirit

Joel

In the midst of a dire warning about the end of the world, the prophet Joel speaks words that were recited generations later by Peter in his first post-Pentecost sermon:

> And afterwards,
>   I will pour out my Spirit on all people.
> Your sons and daughters will prophesy,
>   your old men will dream dreams,
>   your young men will see visions.
> Even on my servants, both men and women,
>   I will pour out my Spirit in those days.
> I will show wonders in the heavens
>   and on the earth,
>   blood and fire and billows of smoke.
> The sun will be turned to darkness
>   and the moon to blood
>   before the coming of the great and dreadful day of the Lord.
> And everyone who calls
>   on the name of the Lord will be saved;
> for on Mount Zion and in Jerusalem
>   there will be deliverance,
>   as the Lord has said,
> even among the survivors
>   whom the Lord calls.
>
> JOEL 2:28–32

The context of this passage is worth noting. Joel spoke warnings about the current state of affairs, with the land of Judah being frequently threatened by incoming armies and invaders. Alongside this political and geographic uncertainty, with threat levels at their highest, Joel also refers to climate issues – famine, floods and crop failure. The people were living under the imminent threat of disease, despair and desolation. They were on the lookout for the end of the world. To make the situation even worse, Joel's prophecy not only concerns the immediate context, but it was also a call to (spiritual) arms (or knees), as these present traumatic and terrifying conditions were only a foretaste of what was to come unless there was wholesale reformation and repentance among the people.

This is a book that recognises the underlying fears of a people – fear of failure, fear of invasion, fear of bad things happening, fear of the absence of God, fear of illness, fear of death. This is a message even for those with a fear of creepy crawlies, as Joel speaks of salvation from the plagues of locusts which were ravaging Judah. It is likely that this is a metaphor for the oncoming onslaught of armies seeking to overthrow the king, but it is still a comforting thought that hope can transcend even the fear of insects and arachnids!

Society was broken and divided, and the people were in the midst of lamenting all that they had lost. They were frightened, and they felt alone. For Joel, his early lament over what was being experienced was only the start of the story. It was only in the recognition of what was going wrong that the Spirit was offered as an alternative, turning the world they knew upside down. The context provided a reality check, into which God injected a vision of hope, both for the present and the future. This hope was contingent on the people (and indeed the whole creation) turning back to God – but the result was a spectacular realigning of the people into the divine flow.

Hope was, and is, found in the receiving of the Holy Spirit, uniting the community with the wider culture and providing the mysterious means by which the kingdom of God can flourish and be enacted afresh. The Holy Spirit was offered to the people indiscriminately. The Spirit was a gift for everyone, regardless of age, gender or race. The Holy Spirit was for all people, regardless of rank, status, intelligence or experience. The implanted hope of the Spirit was a gift that enabled fear to be vanquished and the kingdom of God to transform society. The Spirit of God is the hope of the world.

As a result of this, people would dream new dreams, and their frustration would be refracted into hope and visions of what might be possible. No one is exempt from the possibility of joining in with the mission of God through the Holy Spirit and stepping out of fear into God's promised new land. Everyone is invited, and the whole of creation is able to respond to the divine flow within all things.

In the words of 1990s pop band D:Ream, 'things can only get better'.

The Holy Spirit is the antidote to the fears of contemporary society, just as the Spirit was for Joel in this passage. Through the work of the Holy Spirit, fear is replaced by opportunity. Where there is political unrest, there is the hope of promised unity. Where the climate threatens life, there is the hope of Eden restored. Where there is illness and trauma, there is the hope of healing and the experience of divine comfort.

Crucially, the work of the Spirit transforms a community as well as individuals. This is countercultural for a contemporary reader, but it is important to recognise that the Holy Spirit is not a self-help tool for the individually broken. Instead, the Spirit is the divine force of beauty, grace and love, which transcends brokenness and fear and offers the invitation to participate in a living, loving community of hope. The Spirit is the invitation for humanity to be the transformative answer to fear.

Acts and the Holy Spirit

In Acts 2, Jesus' friends were not in good shape. They had witnessed the crucifixion, albeit from the shadows and sidelines. They had seen the resurrection and had tricky personal conversations with Jesus in light of their actions. Just when things were starting to find a new normal, Jesus suddenly disappeared from them on a cloud (there's the symbol of the Holy Spirit again), promising that they would not be alone. They felt pretty alone at that point, despite what Jesus had said.

They were afraid. They were afraid of being alone. They were afraid that the previous few days were some sort of communal psychotic episode. They were afraid that they would mess up again. They were afraid that without Jesus, everything that they had seen and done would be forgotten. They were afraid for their own safety, especially as the Roman forces were gaining momentum again. They were afraid because they didn't know what was going to happen next. They were afraid because they missed their friends; they were living with the pain and questions that result from suicide, as well as the absence of Jesus. They were afraid because they had had all these experiences and all this training yet still had more questions than answers, and now Jesus wasn't around to help them out.

Luke tells us that this group of frightened, holy people remained together. For ten days they met together and tried to figure out what had happened and what was going to happen next. They jostled about who was going to lead them next. They tried to fix their sense of brokenness by adding more people into their community, but that only increased their vulnerability and the risk of greater fragmentation. Peter tried to jolly people along, but he was just as scared as the rest, and so he just sounded a bit garbled and out of his depth. Again.

They all felt out of place, and so they all stuck together. In an upper room. In Jerusalem.

As good Jews, they met together on the festival day of Shavuot – the Jewish celebration of the wheat harvest – and read the Hebrew scriptures together. Pentecost was a permitted holy day, enabling people to feast together and to give thanks to God for the gifts and provision of another successful harvest.

In New Testament terms, Pentecost was apt, as the celebrations were then marked by provision not of food but of spiritual sustenance. The Spirit brings the implanted hope for the future of the kingdom of God in the world.

As these friends met together, their questions swirling yet their spirituality resting in the rituals and practices they knew and recited year on year, strange things began to happen. Spiritual special effects started to surround them: the sound of wind and the sight of non-burning tongues of fire. The friends began to talk among themselves, the holy, beautiful, terrifying moment made even more chaotic and surreal by the different languages that they were able to speak. The friends who had been hiding out in secret began to make a lot of noise. Their voices rose in volume. They were no longer being subtle.

A crowd began to grow outside of the house. This group of frightened friends lost their anonymity and their isolation, and the Holy Spirit began to infect other people and incite interest in the growing revelry. People heard their own language being spoken as the divine flow began to demonstrate what it meant to be inclusive and universal. People who had felt excluded in the past were now actively hearing words spoken in ways they could understand.

And none of this was happening in the temple grounds. The Holy Spirit had left the building.

Through the Holy Spirit, hope is implanted in hearts and minds. Hope is not confined to boxes, perfume bottles or the temple; hope floods into the lives of the broken and brings restoration, vision and healing.

Some people didn't understand. But the friends did. When the moment had worn off a little, and the crowd had begun to disperse, it didn't take long for the disciples to begin to put into practice their experimental 'holy habits' of discipleship. Their response to the Holy Spirit was a communal method of worship, social action and corporate responsibility:

> They devoted themselves to the apostles' teaching and to fellowship, to the breaking of bread and to prayer. Everyone

was filled with awe at the many wonders and signs performed by the apostles. All the believers were together and had everything in common. They sold property and possessions to give to anyone who had need. Every day they continued to meet together in the temple courts. They broke bread in their homes and ate together with glad and sincere hearts, praising God and enjoying the favour of all the people. And the Lord added to their number daily those who were being saved.

ACTS 2:42–47

'What does this mean?' the crowds asked themselves. The divine flow, the Holy Spirit, invited the crowds into a new narrative of hope amid fear. The crowds were invited to pay attention to a different way of living that was grounded in the love of God for the whole of creation, rather than one that was both individualistic and nationalistic.

The Holy Spirit has left the building. The kingdom of God is right here, right now. Do not fear. Hope is here.

Hope is here and it looks like a fire, bringing new shape and purpose into the journey of life.

Hope is here and it looks like breath, filling every pore and cell with the potential to be life-giving.

Hope is here and it looks like oil, acting like the best doctor's surgery in the world, as people are healed in body, mind and spirit.

Hope is here and it looks like a counsellor: those with poor mental health are invited to know the psychologist Spirit, the bringer of peace.

Hope is here and it pinpoints the holy.

Hope looks like justice for all. It looks like the equal distribution of provision. It looks like a family get-together. It looks like generosity and hospitality, whether served with lobster or jelly and ice cream. It is fundamentally inclusive (not exclusively fundamental). It looks like holy chaos, and it's full of questions and laughter and tears and storytelling, as everyone is treated with dignity and acceptance. It's gloriously messy and graciously free. It feels like falling in love for the first time.

As a consequence of being loved beyond measure, we begin to live and love differently, being marked as a community of people of love, joy, peace, patience, kindness, goodness, faithfulness and self-control. Because, ultimately, that is what hope is – an invitation to be loved by the creative force beneath and within the whole universe and, in turn, to change the world. Whatever description of the Spirit is offered, the overarching message throughout scripture is that the Spirit of God overcomes despair. The age of the Spirit overcomes a culture of fear. In such an age, the whole of creation is invited to discover the love which binds the universe together.

Finding the divine flow of hopeful resistance

The Holy Spirit is everywhere, within everything. The Spirit is the source and the destination, the beginning and the end of all things. The Spirit, the divine flow, is the melody within creation, calling humanity and the created order into a rhythm of life that takes note of the deeper magic (as C.S. Lewis describes it in the Narnia tales). This flow, the Spirit, underpins all things and calls all things into their best existence.

The divine flow brings hope, beauty, grace and love into the most ugly, mean and desperate of places. It can be discovered on city balconies and public squares. It can be heard at the top of an escalator in L'Enfant Plaza. It is present in the tapping of keys on a keyboard and the ping of an email alert. It is within the creaking of arthritic bones and beneath every sob of a broken heart. It is the sound of leaves falling in the autumn, and it is the pulsing of every light ray of the sun. The divine flow breathes life and love – and hope – into all things, a gentle reminder that we are for something bigger than ourselves.

It can take a lifetime to become fully open to and aware of the full force of this divine flow, this Holy Spirit. But there are invitations, glimpses and opportunities to notice God at work and to join in with those holy moments. In a world more shaped by fear than hope, finding ways to rediscover something of the divine flow within all things may well be the greatest task of hopeful resistance open to us.

Over the past two decades, significant shifts in thinking have occurred when it comes to the work of the Spirit and the calling of the church. The Holy Spirit at work in the world inspires the church to respond to what the Spirit is already doing. This inversion of more historic forms of evangelism and mission, where the Christian project was transposed into a (often indigenous) culture, is a seismic shift in both thinking and practice. The invitation is to partner with the Spirit. Church is not itself on mission. Rather, it is the Spirit of God who has a mission, and it is the invitation of the Spirit to get involved with the Spirit's project of bringing forth the kingdom of God.

In many ways, this comes as a relief. By implication, it is not the role of Christians to save the Christian faith. It is not the role of the church to recruit new members, nor to keep renovating itself to be more relevant to the prevailing culture. Instead, it is the task of the church, as individuals as well as corporate groups and wider denominational institutions, to discern the work of the Spirit and to participate in the Spirit's performance of the kingdom of God. This is the calling of hopeful resistance.

It is, however, not without its challenges, not least in the interpretation and practice of diversity and inclusion that is at the heart of the Spirit's work. The Holy Spirit hovered over creation and made all things in the midst of the chaos of the waters (itself a symbol). The Spirit enabled diversity – demonstrated in the great parabolic poem of the tower of Babel. In a dream to Peter in the New Testament, the Spirit testified to opening the kingdom of God to anyone who is intrigued by it. Much of Paul's teaching and letter writing were on the theme of being united, reconciled and healed. Through the Holy Spirit, Revelation 21 says that the nations too are healed. The divine flow, uncontainable, wild and liberating, must also be good news for all.

Hopeful resistance turns the lives of individuals upside down. More significantly, the Spirit works towards the transformation of society. The Holy Spirit, present and at work in the world today, is the primary vehicle for the coming kingdom of God among us, for the benefit of the whole of humanity and the whole created order. The work of the Holy Spirit means that the answer to fear, despair and trauma is not apathy but action. Such action is in partnership with the Spirit. It is not all done in our own strength, nor do we have the option of assuming that this is just the way things are now. Life is tough and might not get better in the way that we want. The world is broken, and some broken things don't get fixed. Things hurt and it's important not to let those emotions fade before their time. But in the tough, broken and hurting places, the Spirit is also breathing a vision of life that requires courage to bring to fruition and that brings hope and justice to the whole world.

If only we would take the time to pay attention to what is already around us.

Breaking the law

In the cold, dank, concrete streets of London, a small group of subversive friends are attempting to help people take notice of what has always been around them. Yarnbombing is the practice of knitting a covering for an inanimate object, as a peaceful protest aimed at helping people to discover afresh the beauty that surrounds them. A phone box in Westminster got a telephone tea cosy. A security barrier becomes less imposing when crocheted. Lampposts and trees were given scarves. And so the practice grew. 'Oranges and Lemons' appeared at the door of the bell towers referenced in the children's rhyme. Knitted sea creatures were placed alongside their embalmed real-life inspiration in the Natural History Museum.

Yarnbombing began as a subversive prank to enable people to stop, to pay attention and to notice beauty. It is also a key part of the art of 'crafitivism'. Developed by social action campaigner Sarah Corbett, craftivism uses creative objects and activities to challenge injustice. In *How to be a Craftivist* (Unbound, 2017), she writes:

> The world is amazing. There is so much loveliness in nature… but I know I can make it even more beautiful and more kind and more fair… [I could] channel my anger at injustice and passion for a better world into creative objects and activities. And those crafted objects can then help play a part in tackling the root causes of injustice and help create long-lasting positive change.

So it came to pass that I think I might have broken the law. With the desire for institutional and social change in mind, I might be guilty of trespass. I collaborated in a national craftivism campaign to challenge racism and the flawed immigration policy in the UK by displaying a knitted 'all are welcome' banner on the railings of our local railway station. As crimes go, it's not that impressive, but it served as a creative reminder to commuters of inclusion, hospitality and beauty that is not predicated on political affiliation or policy.

Hope is an act of resistance, partnering with the divine flow, the Spirit, to challenge injustice and to bring life, beauty, grace and love into the world, one stitch at a time. The Spirit crafts a new world order into being and invites us to join in.

Hopeful resistance does not, however, rely solely on gimmick. It requires prayerful attentiveness, courage and discernment. This is, after all, all about the kingdom of God as opposed to individual egos.

The Holy Spirit is a vital and revitalising partner in the mission of God. The Holy Spirit helps people notice what has been here all along and invites us to be part of the next chapter.

Hope looks like a bowling ball. In south Wales, a church purchased land on an industrial estate, on which it built a ten-pin bowling alley. It now employs people who would otherwise have difficulty finding work, especially those with life-limiting conditions. Any profit from the business gets redirected to support other ministries in the same industrial estate: the food bank, clothing store and school uniform repair centre. Within that complex of buildings, a broken society is challenged and the needs of the community are met.

Hope looks like a carpentry workshop. In Scotland, a church worker noticed that there was a need to work with young people, especially men, who left school unskilled. He turned his garage into a workshop, found a few tools in a skip and began to teach himself woodwork. Now working under the brand 'The Bearded Woodworker', the garage has become a creative hub for people to learn carpentry skills in community and to prioritise the refurbishment and repurposing of materials found in skips, picked up from flotsam and jetsam on the beach or donated to them directly. Young men in one of the most deprived areas of the UK are encouraged and equipped to find the beauty in broken things.

Hope looks like a choir. In England, a performing arts teacher wanted to find a way to enable people who had been affected by cancer to meet in a safe environment. Their partner was undergoing treatment for cancer at the time, and they wanted the opportunity to meet with people outside of a clinical setting. They began to advertise a community choir. Three years on, the choir now has over 150 members and meets weekly to sing together. Each term, their performances raise money for cancer charities. Each performance prioritises music that reflects the liturgical year, mixing the sacred and the secular while finding a safe place to share stories of hope and loss. Together, broken people are discovering their voice.

Hope looks like an adapted specialist classroom. Further south in England, a family living with the impact of autism and attention deficit disorder find it increasingly difficult to attend worship. As their participation in church reduced, so did their ability to engage with many social situations. The family became more and more isolated, and in a vicious circle the special needs of the family thus worsened. It took a while for this to be noticed, but a change in minister and the addition to the congregation of another family with similar experiences led to a project specifically designed to help families impacted by special educational needs (SEN). A sensory room was added to the youth area. A chaplaincy was developed with the youth club, so those with additional needs could be supported in personally relevant ways. The church began a dementia-care programme, further developing the skills of the whole congregation in hospitality and welcome. Plans remain in place for future work with SEN specialists in the local school and some respite provision for child carers. Not broken so much as living with different life experiences, the Holy Spirit nudged a community into being a place of welcome to all.

Hope looks like a pot of tea and a plate of biscuits. A small village church, on the brink of unsustainable presence in their community, discovered the gift of opening the church doors regularly throughout the week. They began to offer simple refreshments – tea, coffee and biscuits – but also a safe place for people to be listened to. Worship attendance has not increased, but the reputation of the church has, as has the church's understanding of the local community, its needs and where help can be found if needed. The church took its own sense of failure and dislocation from the wider community and made it the catalyst for its rediscovery of God's calling for them.

Hope looks like a stocked pantry and a hot meal. A congregation was approached by a local school, because children were arriving to school on Monday tired and hungry. Although a breakfast club was provided during the week, this did not happen at weekends. Students in low-income households were spending the weekend hungry, as there was no food at home. As a result, the congregation now provides take-home bags of food for vulnerable families to prepare meals over the weekend. In addition, the congregation provides meals throughout the school holidays. This has recently evolved further, as someone noticed that the school uniforms of some of these vulnerable pupils were less than adequate. As a result, there is now a uniform exchange at the church, and a weekly sewing group offer a uniform repair service. A small team of people, responding to a recognised need in a local school, then begins to notice some of the other interrelated issues and responds accordingly. They follow the flow to see where it may lead them next.

Each of these examples shows what happens when people are attentive to the work of the Spirit bringing healing, restoration and hope into broken spaces and places beyond themselves. They demonstrate what happens when people rise up, live courageously and creatively, and say 'yes' to what they discern is something of the Spirit nudging them forth. They show what is possible when brokenness is not taken for granted, when anger becomes action and when partnering with the divine flow encourages the stepping out of comfort zones. When this happens, beauty and grace and love are noticed in the midst of dereliction and depravity, the spaces everyone else has given up on. The world is turned upside down.

The Holy Spirit never gives up. The Spirit always protects, always trusts, always hopes, always perseveres. Christian mission has left the building, because the Spirit was never confined to it in the first place. The Holy Spirit is not, and cannot remain, a hidden inconvenience, an unnecessary flourish of salvation history. The Spirit is the ultimate practitioner of mission, empowering individuals and communities to discover afresh their unique calling as people of God. It is through the Spirit that brokenness and vulnerability become the vehicles for personal and social transformation. As noted in the previous chapter, the worst thing is never the last thing. But it may be the catalyst for something new to emerge: a resur-rection of sorts.

The Holy Spirit is love where there is hate, beauty in the midst of brokenness, grace in the gutter, healing in pain, hope in despair.

Philosopher David Foster Wallace, in a speech just prior to his death, spoke of this Spirit, this divine flow, in this way:

> If you've really learned how to think, how to pay attention, then you will know you have other options. It will be within your power to experience a crowded, loud, slow, consumer-hell-type situation as not only meaningful but sacred, on fire with the same force that lit the stars – compassion, love, the sub-surface unity of all things.

The Spirit calls the whole of humanity, alongside the whole of creation, to pay attention. It doesn't need the gimmicks of *The Washington Post* to achieve its purpose, although such an experiment helps to raise the question of where beauty is to be discovered. If we pay attention and develop methods and means by which we can enter the divine flow, we will begin to notice beauty and grace and love in our midst with the same force that lit the stars. We will risk becoming the change agents who enable others to join in with those things that bring the kingdom of God into being in the present moment, whether or not there is a concert violinist performing on a street corner.

The Spirit of God is bringing life and beauty into being, and it is our calling to take notice and to join in. This is our invitation to hopeful, holy resistance: to turn the world upside down.

Questions for reflection

- What word, symbol, metaphor or image would you use to describe the Holy Spirit? Why?

- Where have you seen the Holy Spirit at work in your own life?

- Where have you seen the Holy Spirit at work in your local community or in the wider world?

- The Holy Spirit brings dreams and visions for a better world. What dream or vision has the Holy Spirit instilled in you? What do you need to do about it?

- What does hopeful resistance look and feel like for you?

7

Dagen Högertrafik

I urge you to live a life worthy of the calling you have received. Be completely humble and gentle; be patient, bearing with one another in love. Make every effort to keep the unity of the Spirit through the bond of peace. There is one body and one Spirit, just as you were called to one hope when you were called; one Lord, one faith, one baptism; one God and Father of all, who is over all and through all and in all.

EPHESIANS 4:1–6

If you are brave enough to love people, you're going to get your heart broken. If you're courageous enough to care about something, you're going to get disappointed. If you're creative and innovative enough to try new things, you're going to fail. So the bravest among us are always the broken-hearted, because they took a chance.

Brené Brown, *Rising Strong* (Vermilion, 2015)

Turning around

On Sunday 3 September 1967, a revolution began: Dagen Högertrafik.

At 5.00 am on this wistful Sunday morning, the traffic across Sweden stopped. For the following six hours, the cars on the roads carefully manoeuvred their way around and began driving on the opposite side of the road.

After this brainchild of a project that had taken a decade to be agreed and a further four years to implement, Sweden was never to be the same again. The preceding years had included a government-sponsored re-education programme across the whole country. Advertising and instructions were printed on milk cartons – and even underwear. A nationwide song contest was held, as a theme song was chosen to launch the auspicious morning. The national infrastructure needed to be changed, as the contemporary equivalent of £700 million was invested in the road and transportation system, changing everything from traffic lights to switching the sides of the bus where the doors opened.

At 5.00 am, everyone changed direction. A report of the day from a local mayor stated, 'It caused a brief, monumental traffic jam, but Swedish people experienced a revolution for just a few hours which has changed our world for the better and for the good.'

The reasoning behind the revolution has been proven to be a little flawed. While driving on the right puts Sweden in the same direction of travel as its Scandinavian neighbours, and thus made border crossing easier, the more potent suggestion that right-hand drivers had fewer accidents has, alas, proved inaccurate.

What does it take to turn a nation around? A vision, an underwear campaign, a good tune, £700 million and six hours of patience!

While a delightful story in itself, this model of change perhaps also offers us a final insight into how we might find God in a culture of fear today. Images from Sweden in 1967 show either a carnival atmosphere of street parties and celebration or a chaotic scene of trauma and panic, often described as being like a war zone. Is a culture of chaos one of celebration or one of terror? I suspect that it was both, depending on which side of the road you were on.

If living and loving in the 21st century is going to achieve anything other than the survival of the fittest, richest, loudest or most celebrated, perhaps we need a few more revolutionaries and revolutions in our communities. This is, and always has been, the calling of the people of God. The church has always been called to repent, to turn around, to change direction. We need people who, like the ancient prophets, call people to account and demonstrate that another world is possible; people who, like Jesus, are willing to call people to repentance (literally to turn around), even at the risk of death; people who, noticing the work of the Spirit, find a different course of action than the one to which they are most accustomed.

There is a gift in the language of revolution or repentance, because both can indicate the need for a change of direction. This is not some self-help change of life direction in order to be more fulfilled, although that might be an accidental consequence. Theologically, repentance is about a change of direction in order to centre oneself and the community around God once again; to get back on course with worship and relationship to the creator; to be prepared to give up self for the benefit of the (often excluded) other.

It is now something of a cliché to say that the local church, when working well, is the hope of the world. The local church is neither immune from the crippling anxiety humanity is becoming so familiar with, nor is it working particularly well – incumbered as it is by ageing and declining congregations, the burdens of bureaucracy and the challenges of a secularising agenda. Yet we are still called to be revolutionaries of hope.

In order to live life hopefully, who and what might God be calling the church to become for the 21st century and beyond? What might our change of direction need to be? How might the church be the hope of the world, rather than an anathema of a bygone era? Crucially, what might our confession and our repentance need to be?

It's worth returning briefly to the theme of exile, introduced in chapter 2. According to Walter Brueggemann, one of the key gifts of the metaphor of exile is the ability to grieve, mourn and lament. If humanity is to be marked by hope, then there is a vital and critical need to reclaim and rediscover the power of lament and confession. There is catharsis in recognising the pain and despair of the current situation, railing against it and being authentic about the tragedy of the present situation. There is also opportunity to confess corporate and personal complicity in getting into this mess in the first place, a recognition of collusion in the powers and practices that have produced the current outcome. Freedom can be found in the honest articulation of the guilt, fear, shame, despair, anger and sadness felt within contemporary society. The challenge is to trust that God is big and strong enough to take our insults, and to trust that even in the midst of pain and confusion, there is still something of a relationship with God to fight for, as well as something to fight against.

Seven months before he died, with raspy vocals that frustrated him, the music legend Johnny Cash reluctantly recorded a song of lament, entitled 'Hurt'. It was a cover of a song originally performed by thrash metal band Nine Inch Nails. The song, coupled with a profound video filmed in the decaying ruins of one of Cash's homes, is a powerful poem of lament and loss. In 2011, the track was awarded 'best song and video of all time' by *NME* magazine, and still features in the *Time* magazine list of all-time greatest songs. There is a need for laments such as this, which can transform the performer as well as the listener. In the context of death, despair and decay, in the right hands (the song needed Cash to perform it), laments enable there to be beauty, craft and artistry, even hope, when they are authentic, raw and visceral.

The church in the west in the 21st century is being called to change direction – to let loose with our grief, frustration and lament, and to begin to forge something new in the ashes and embers of what once was strong, but which has crumbled to dust beneath the pressures of ideology, intransigence, inequality and division. The church is being called to repent of the perception and veneer of having everything altogether and all sorted. Christian communities are instead discovering the liberation that comes from being authentic, vulnerable and honest about struggles, debates, despair and decline.

This is nothing new – from exodus to exile, resurrection to religious persecutions, the Bible shows us a God who calls on the people to change direction and to change the world. And for some of those people, the change of direction meant giving up everything that they owned and stood for, in order for the Spirit of God to begin to fashion something new. Like the Ephesians in the book of Revelation, the church is being wooed and called back to its first love, and to prioritise the minority and the mission field over and against management and ministry. These are challenging times and will require lament and confession as well as dreams and innovations.

Alongside lament and confession, the revolution also includes parties – parties for those who have fought and won; parties for those who have fought and lost; parties for those who have stood the test of time, but who now need to stop and take stock. Be this about personal health battles or the long-running contestation over chapel buildings, may the church be a place of parties and balloons and buckets of ice, recognising the people and the stories that are imbued into the very brickwork.

Critically, for some places, there is a need to repent because a change of direction has been fought against for too long. Dreams have disappeared into an Ecclesiastes-style vapour. Ric Stott is an artist and Methodist minister. For one of his installations during Lent, he made 40 clay figurines. They looked like the children's TV character Morph, albeit in a sitting pose. These 40 characters were then placed in different locations around the city in which Ric lived and left for the Lent period, to see what would happen to them. Around Easter, Ric returned to the places where the characters had been left. Almost half had survived their ordeal; some were tainted with pollutants, such as exhaust fumes; some were affected rather profoundly by the environmental changes wrought upon them, seemingly melting into their surroundings as the rain eroded them away. One, left in a local skatepark, had become enshrined by the local young people, who had built it a shelter and regularly offered it food. One, devastatingly, had been deliberately stamped on and destroyed – its remnants squished into the pavement, the soleprints still visible.

Most tellingly, however, was the one that was placed in a local chapel. Whereas all the other retrieved characters had in some way become part of the surroundings in which they were placed, the figure placed in the church remained untouched and unnoticed. It is perhaps no surprise that this happened, but it is a sad indictment of communities who are unable to be transformed by their context and to transform those selfsame communities in different ways. As the chapter on Jesus being involved in the muck and mire of life suggests, part of the calling of the church is about participating in the wider community, rather than being a place of preservation and safety from it. The challenge for us in the 21st century is to be brave and bold, and to risk giving up some of our territory, if we are not, in fact, doing the work of the kingdom of God in our midst.

Hope will not be found in the tired and the worn-out. Exhaustion is not a gift of the Spirit. We need a change of direction that enables communities of people to be released from the burdens of caretaking inappropriate buildings and physical assets, and instead calls people back into a relationship with God and with each other that is about 'learning the unforced rhythms of grace' (Matthew 11:29, MSG), which are placed upon God's people 'lightly'. Some of us need to have the confidence and the humility to know that enough is enough and that the most hopeful thing we can do is to stop, throw a party and know that this is the end of a job well done. Good and faithful servants.

Some people need to find their voice and to share those things that are hurting and decaying – be it buildings or bones. In a UK context, where mainstream institutional ministry is often spent being a good landlord to the wishes and whims of our tenants, rather than excellence in Christ-centred, Spirit-filled, hope-fuelled worship, there is a dissonance about who the church is for. Is the church primarily a safety net for the believer, or is it the emergency response team for the excluded, marginalised and broken? Does the church exist for itself, or is it a community of people which exists for the sole benefit of those who are outside of its current reach and rescue? Whose hope is it?

A change of direction is needed, so that mission continues to be about getting Jesus-centred people out of our buildings, not making sure we get enough people into them to pay the overhead costs. Church is not (only) about what happens on a Sunday morning. Hope-filled communities will challenge the insidiousness of the culture of fear but recognise when God turns up at any time in the week. The church is being called to repent of the notion that God is somehow at our beck and call, wish and whim, and to realise the opposite is true – that the church is filled with people who are so in tune with the heart of God that we take the opportunities afforded to us to bring life and light into the bleak and meaningless places of a lost, hurting, shamed and hopeless world.

In what has become possibly the most broadcast sermon in history, Bishop Michael Curry at the wedding of the Duke and Duchess of Sussex spoke about the need to 'think and imagine' what the world would look like if love got in the way of all things:

> [The] way of unselfish, sacrificial, redemptive love can change lives and it can change this world. If you don't believe me, just stop and think and imagine a world where love is the way. Imagine our homes and families when this way of love is the way. Imagine neighbourhoods and communities where love is the way. Imagine our governments and nations where love is the way. Imagine business and commerce when this love is the way. Imagine this tired old world when love is the way.
>
> No child would go to bed hungry in such a world as that. When love is the way, we will let justice roll down like a mighty stream and righteousness like an ever-flowing brook. When love is the

way, poverty will become history. When love is the way, the earth will be a sanctuary. When love is the way, we will lay down our swords and shields down by the riverside to study war no more. When love is the way, there's plenty good room – plenty good room – for all of God's children.

If church is the community of Jesus-knowing, Spirit-filled, love-conquered people, the church today is being called to a change of direction, one that is about offering hope to royalty as well as ragamuffins. Finding God in a culture of fear is in part about becoming a community of people who are open-hearted and open-handed to all.

Christian hope is one of co-creation and collaboration with the divine flow. Hope is what happens when love gets in the way.

Imagine

Imagine a place where people talk about God's presence and God's absence, and lost keys, and diagnoses, and therapy appointments, and family and questions, as a natural day-to-day occurrence that is honest and full of truth, and no one feels as though they have to compete. What if church happened when we told stories of hope in adversity and of the underdog being the chosen one, for such a time as this? Imagine a place where personal testimonies were filled with the true reality and cost of pain, but also with the undiluted hope that the worst thing is never the last thing. But the worst thing can still be spoken, named, owned. And in so doing, it loses the power of being a mark of fear, shame, guilt and doubt, and instead becomes the words that build understanding and knowing and life and love and… well, hope.

Imagine a place full of questions and conversation, not easy answers, perhaps no answers at all. A place where evangelism isn't an argument, but is about sharing life together. Amid this dialogue, it also becomes a community of people who are not afraid to wrestle with the scriptures and to disagree on matters of interpretation, because we are all learners of the gospel and none of us have it all sorted out yet. What if our change of direction doesn't expect some theological elitism from our leaders but rather expects every member, from the toddler to the great-grandparent, to be hungry for more theology not less of it? Hope doesn't come without a fight, after all. Hope comes from engaging with the difficult parts of life and through mending relationships and healing wounds. Hope comes alongside our scars and transforms our misunderstandings. Finding God in a culture of fear means exposing fear to scrutiny and discovering that knowledge and relationships, not ignorance and exclusion, are the currency of change.

Imagine a place where inclusion is natural, not extraordinary – and where we're done with labels because it's people who matter to God. Hope is diverse not divisive.

Imagine a place where the worship attendance is bigger than the local slimming club, who rent the back room several days a week, because we have something to say about the importance and gift of our bodies – with wrinkles, stretch marks and scars intact – because our bodies tell our stories as much as our words. A place where a change of direction means that we are able to celebrate our bodies and to treat them as temples, rather than continuing to buy in to the quasi-Augustinian practices of body-shaming. Hope is embodied resistance.

Imagine a church that is not run by committees alone, but which spends at least an equal amount of time in Bible study, prayer and meaningful conversation together. Hope is a spiritual discipline.

Imagine a place where people are so at home that jumping on the furniture or running and dancing is recognised as a natural part of an individual's spiritual development, without an age restriction on behaviour. The church is being called to repent of the notion that 'proper behaviour' is a mark of true discipleship, and instead it is discovering that being a proactive and participatory member of an outward-focused community of people is the means of changing the world. Hope is playful and recreative.

In times of despair and fear, the most powerful tool for proactive and prophetic action is to be found in the midst of prayer. Imagine that within the place of active chaos, there is also a place of deep stillness and quiet – an oasis of peace and life in the midst of despair. A place which teaches and practices meditation and mindfulness. A place of seeking the Source. A place where inactivity and being fully present is the counterbalance to the risk of hyperactively responding to every glimmer of hopelessness. Hope tunes out the noise.

Imagine a place where the kettle is always on, because there's always someone at the door needing a brew or a bath. Or both. A place where hospitality is radical and means more than stale coffee and custard creams served in crockery saved up from the 1950s. Hope is open-hearted.

Jesus ate dinner with people. As we noted earlier, Jesus ate with his friends as well as with undesirables. Perhaps he was on to something. Hospitality is a silver bullet in the development of communities. Sociologist Cody Delistraty, in the paper 'The importance of eating together', notes that families who no longer eat together have a 'quantifiable negative effect both physically and psychologically'. Delistraty goes on to identify the following themes from his research in the USA:

- Students who do not regularly eat with their parents are significantly more likely to be truant at school.
- Children who do not eat dinner with their parents at least twice a week are 40 percent more likely to be overweight compared to those who do.
- Children who do eat dinner with their parents five or more days a week have less trouble with drugs and alcohol, eat healthier, show

    better academic performance and report being closer with their
    parents than children who eat dinner with their parents less often.
- The best prescription to prevent eating disorders in teenagers is
regular family dinners which host a positive atmosphere.

It is not a surprise that in Jesus-centred communities, table
fellowship and table talk are vital for good order and social
development. Feasting together, around a table, is an equaliser
where everyone is welcome. It's a key reason why providing food
is so important in some more popular programmes, such as Alpha
and Messy Church. Eating together breaks down prejudice, builds
relationship, sustains the body and provides the context for human
flourishing. Hope breaks bread and offers it around the table.

Imagine a place of invitations, open to the most weird as well as the
people as weird as us. The church is being called to offer hope to
those who are misfits in society; to offer an open table where all are
welcome. A consequence of church growth has often been the gentrification of members, who in turn often unconsciously oppress those
of lesser standing. Finding God in an age of fear is not about self-
promotion. Indeed, it may well be the latter. Imagine if church was
not about the bettering of social standing but was about celebrating
complexity and diversity and messed-up people. Church isn't then a
place of being 'fixed', but is a place of being accepted. Hope doesn't
expect that everything broken will be fixed like it was before.

Imagine a place where there's always a fight to join the washing-up
rota, because who doesn't like playing with bubbles? Plus, all the
best parties finish in the kitchen.

Imagine a place where those under the age of 45 make all the policy
decisions, so that we future-proof our legacy rather than preserve our
personal preferences. Finding God in a culture of fear is about letting
go of power and enabling people with a different world view to offer
us a renewed vision of hope and a change of direction. In many of our
churches, however, power has been gripped for so long by so few that

there is only a single generation left in church buildings. Crucially, we need to lament for the people that we have lost and pushed away, and, by doing so, effectively signed our death warrant. Hope raises a lament for what was lost and will never be again.

Imagine a place where we commission as many people as social activists as we do Sunday school teachers. A place where fear is tackled by community engagement and prophetic action. A place where another world is possible, and where the church is at the cutting edge of where that happens. In a context where global climate change and the threat of plastic to our environment are perhaps the greatest threats to humanity's existence, the church has the opportunity to be a world leader in creation care, recycling, sustainable living and community gardening. After all, gardens play host to good news. Hope changes the world. Sometimes this requires wellies.

Imagine what church could be if creativity were the key to our connectedness with God and each other. Imagine a place where our worship spaces become studios for artists and wordsmiths. A place where spirituality is multisensory and where beauty beats cynicism. Hope is always creative.

Imagine a place where we no longer count stuff, because we've realised that counting people and counting the collection are bad measures of social change and world impact. A change of direction is needed that begins to measure our social impact and our global footprint. These don't have to be complicated; they could be biblical. We could begin to measure how loving, joyful, patient, peaceful, kind, good, faithful, gentle and self-controlled we are – and where these are then influencing other areas of the wider culture around and about us. How do we measure what happens when love gets in the way?

Imagine what church could be if it became a place of proactive, participatory, prophetic people – people willing to lament the loss and shame of the past, but resilient and courageous in the face of a culture of fear.

In the Dagen Högertrafik, it took Sweden six hours to change the world – or at least to change direction. May we be the revolutionaries who change the direction of travel, grounded in the hope found in God's character, Jesus' example, the Spirit's inspiration, an ancient/future promise and our calling as the people of God, as we notice the Spirit of God calling us to much, much more and, in the great paradox of the kingdom of God, much, much less.

The resistance of Christian hope is only just getting started!

> How can we be hopeless? There's too much work to do.
> Dorothy Day

Questions for discussion

- Where have you experienced the local church as the hope of the world?

- Why is lament an important part of repentance and change?

- Is the church primarily for the benefit of its members, or for those who do not yet know Jesus?

- How do you respond to these imaginations of what the church might be in the future? Which strikes a chord with you? Which do you struggle with?

- What might you need to be prepared to let go of to see this vision become a reality?

- What would you add?

Epilogue

Faith, hope and love

No matter what I say, what I believe, and what I do, I'm bankrupt without love.

> Love never gives up.
> Love cares more for others than for self.
> Love doesn't want what it doesn't have.
> Love doesn't strut,
> Doesn't have a swelled head,
> Doesn't force itself on others,
> Isn't always 'me first',
> Doesn't fly off the handle,
> Doesn't keep score of the sins of others,
> Doesn't revel when others grovel,
> Takes pleasure in the flowering of truth,
> Puts up with anything,
> Trusts God always,
> Always looks for the best,
> Never looks back,
> But keeps going to the end…

We don't yet see things clearly. We're squinting in a fog, peering through a mist. But it won't be long before the weather clears and the sun shines bright! We'll see it all then, see it all as clearly as God sees us, knowing him directly just as he knows us!

But for right now, until that completeness, we have three things to do to lead us towards that consummation: *Trust steadily in*

God, hope unswervingly, love extravagantly. And the best of the three is love.

1 CORINTHIANS 13:3–7, 12–13 (MSG, italics added)

Okay. So what's next?

Transforming
lives and communities

Christian growth and understanding of the Bible

Resourcing individuals, groups and leaders in churches for their own spiritual journey and for their ministry

Church outreach in the local community

Offering two programmes that churches are embracing to great effect as they seek to engage with their local communities and transform lives

Teaching Christianity in primary schools

Working with children and teachers to explore Christianity creatively and confidently

Children's and family ministry

Working with churches and families to explore Christianity creatively and bring the Bible alive   **parenting for faith**

Visit **brf.org.uk** for more information on BRF's work

brf.org.uk